THE MARGINS OF THE CITY

Popular Cultural Studies

Series editors: Justin O'Connor, Steve Redhead and Derek Wynne

The Manchester Institute for Popular Culture was set up in order to promote theoretical and empirical research in the area of contemporary popular culture, both within the University and in conjunction with local, national and international agencies. The Institute is currently engaged in two major comparative research projects around aspects of consumption and popular culture in the City. The Institute also runs a number of postgraduate research programmes, with a particular emphasis on ethnographic work. The series intends to reflect all aspects of the Institute's activities. Current theoretical debates within the field of popular culture will be explored within an empirical context. Much of the research is undertaken by young researchers actively involved in their chosen fields of study, allowing an awareness of the issues and an attentiveness to actual developments often lacking in standard academic writings on the subject. The series will also reflect the working methods of the Institute, emphasising a collective research effort and the regular presentation of work-in-progress to the Institute's research seminars. The series hopes, therefore, both to push forward the debates around popular culture, urban regeneration and postmodern social theory whilst introducing an ethnographic and contextual basis for such debates.

Titles already published

Rave Off: Politics and Deviance in Contemporary Youth Culture.
The Passion and the Fashion: Football Fandom in the New Europe.
The Lads in Action: Social Process in an Urban Youth Subculture
Hosts and Champions: Soccer Cultures, National Identities and the USA World Cup
Game Without Frontiers: Football, Identity and Modernity
The Margins of the City: Gay Men's Urban Lives

(Cover photograph: Trevor Paul)

The Margins of the City

Gay men's urban lives

edited by

Stephen Whittle

Published by
Arena
Ashgate Publishing Limited
Gower House
Croft Road
Aldershot
Hants GU11 3HR
England

Ashgate Publishing Company
Old Post Road
Brookfield
Vermont 05036
USA

British Library Cataloguing in Publication Data

The Margins of the City: Gay Men's Urban Lives.
(Popular Cultural Studies)
    I. Whittle, Stephen II. Series
    306.766

ISBN 1 85742 201 5 (Hardback)
ISBN 1 85742 202 3 (Paperback)

Printed and Bound in Great Britain by
Athenaeum Press Ltd, Newcastle upon Tyne.

Contents

Marginal Issues

Maps and Diagrams

Preface

Postmodern (or multinational) space is not merely a cultural ideology or fantasy, but has genuine (and socio-economic) reality as a third great expansion of capitalism around the globe (after the earlier expansions of the national market and the older imperialist system, which each had their own cultural specificity and generated new types of space appropriate to their dynamics) .... We cannot [therefore] return to aesthetic practices elaborated on the basis of historical situations and dilemmas which are no longer ours .... the conception of space that has been developed here suggests that a model of political culture appropriate to our own situation will necessarily have to raise spatial issues as its fundamental organizing concern.
(Jameson, 1984, in Soja, E.W., (1989) *Postmodern Geographies*, Verso, London)

In our cities we mix COMMERCE with CULTURE and PLEASURE. That close affinity is what cities are all about. (Caeser Pelli - Architect)

The authors

Stephen Whittle, School of Law, Manchester Metropolitan University, Hathersage Road, Manchester M13 0EP, United Kingdom.

Paul Hindle, Department of Geography, Salford University, Manchester, M5 4WT, United Kingdom.

Hans Almgren, Department of Geography, Rutgers State University, New Brunswick, New Jersey, NJ 08903, USA.

Anne Marie Bouthillette, Department of Geography, University of British Columbia, #217-1984 West Mall, Vancouver, British Columbia, Canada V6T 1Z2.

Marc Lewis, ex Department of Geography, University of Newcastle Upon Tyne, United Kingdom.

Richard Fay, Centre for English Language Studies and Education (CELSE), University of Manchester, Oxford Road, Manchester M13 9PL, United Kingdom.

Leslie Cox, Centre for English Language Studies and Education (CELSE), University of Manchester, Oxford Road, Manchester M13 9PL, United Kingdom.

David Bell, Geography Division, School of Sciences, Staffordshire University, Leek Road, Stoke on Trent, ST4 2DF, United Kingdom.

Wouter Geurtsen, Department of Leisure Studies, University of Tilberg, Room S155, PO Box 90153, 5000 LE Tilburg, The Netherlands.

Jon Binnie, Department of Geography, University College London, 26 Bedford Way, London WC1H 0AP, United Kingdom.

Introduction

Members of the United Kingdom's Parliament have just voted (February 1994) that the age of consent for consensual sex acts between gay men should be lowered to eighteen years old. Unfortunately over this apparent victory for the liberal face of democracy, there hangs a cloud. Is this really a victory or is it in fact for those gay men who have battled for over 30 years for the same rights to make love as their heterosexual counterparts, a further defeat? Whatever it is, it is a 'victory' which does not bring either equality or inclusion. Gay men, along with their sexual preferences are not being accepted into lawful society as such, the legislation merely means that fewer of them are likely to be physically removed from society and incarcerated because of whom they love. They may still be socially excluded. This theme of exclusion whilst apparently being included, is what this book is about.

It is a book about place and about the infraction of space, the exploration of new territories and falling off the edge of the world - it was only when we landed that we discovered we were on the edge of the middle of our cities. We entered the Twilight Zone.

The geography of the twilight zone of the city has been a major academic area of study throughout the last three decades. We have obsessively looked at the decay and decline of the areas of land, marginal to the city centre, yet not quite the suburbs. But why? The very nature of the 'zone of urban transition' is that nothing happened there, except its slow degeneration into becoming the 'wastelands' - empty and unused warehouses, land into car parks, and a descent into urban places of fear, crime and the terror of the unknown.

For some of us, our fascination went beyond an academic interest: these were the places we haunted, these were the spaces we knew intimately, in which we met our friends and lovers and in which we 'lived' our lives. As geographers (by which I mean all those of us who study the relationship between 'man' and the environment) we knew that other places were far more attractive, but as 'queer geographers' we knew this was where 'our place' was, where our places are!

We hope in this book to contribute to a new geography of the twilight zone, to show that some of us have always lived there, it need not be a space of decline but can now be a space of renewal, and from that renewal there are lessons to be learned by metropolises throughout the world. If you give the margins of our cities to those who want them (and it may well be that they have no choice as they are not wanted elsewhere) then they will make a place out of that space. Lesbians and gay men have done that, not just in San Francisco, but also in Manchester, London, Amsterdam, New York, Toronto and even in 'lowly' Newcastle upon Tyne.

The studies in this collection look at how gay men in particular have made themselves a home within our cities: how they have centralised themselves within our urban environments, and how they have made themselves belong, be important and become essential to the economies of our cities, particularly to the night time economies. By becoming key ingredients in the city's night life, they have gained a foothold on the steps to local power. This has not come easily, and though now important, they have not necessarily gained a place from which they are heard.

Postmodernist theory has seemingly replaced the singularity of political and social theories with a multiplicity and plurality of voices, all of which have truth and validity. This has been achieved by rejecting both the essentialist dichotomies of the liberal theories of the rational enlightenment and the idea that power constructs are essential to the fabric of society. This rejection apparently makes it possible for those who are non-powerful to have a voice for their own truths.

However as Jon Binnie points out in his final chapter in this book, those of us in the Academy, who in our personal lives have experienced 'outsiderness', find that within the institution we are also marginalised. I had an experiential suspicion that only a few powerful voices are actually being heard. The remainder of us are marginalised by our subjects of study which are literally 'beyond the pale'. Sex is still a dirty word.

A deconstruction of power roles within discourses around lesbian and gay lifestyles has not given the means to speak to many, but has only given voice to those who have access to, and the power to use, tools of communication. It is important, in any discussion of voice, to remember that either printing whether it be by photocopier or press, phones, video and television or film and screen access are still, proportionally, available to only the very few.

Very few lesbians, gay men or others marginalised by the nature of their gender or sexual lifestyle choices have access to power. Even if they do they rarely feel able to use that to speak of the issues that marginalise them. The contributors to this book have recognised that they are in a 'powerful' position as members of the Academy, and have used that to try and present some more voices.

It is hoped that this book will give others in the Academy the strength to follow the commitment of the contributors, who have all taken risks and who are 'outing' themselves through their contributions.

The papers, here, are divided into three sections. The first: Manchester, 'It's Queer Up North', looks at the city's Gay Village, its development, its history and its issues - issues which go beyond the gaining of space, but what that means in terms of the place of safety in our theorizing of lesbian and gay concerns. The second: 'Tales of the Cities', has three chapters which consider the development of gay places and communities in the cities of Toronto, Newcastle upon Tyne and New York. Newcastle is the 'odd man out', in that it has not seen the regenerative effects that gay men have brought to Jackson Heights in New York and Cabbagetown in Toronto. But as a city which in itself is on the margins of a country, it illustrates the isolation and poverty of choice that double marginalisation can bring. When Marc Lewis, its author, discusses the lack of facilities available for those with other sexual lifestyles beyond those of being 'straight gay or lesbian', we see a multiple marginalisation process taking place. This draws our attention to what it means to be multiply marginalised, and leads us to the third section of the book. 'Marginal Issues' is where we have considered that multiple marginalisation and its theorisation. David Bell considers Bisexuality and its centrality to those issues, Richard Fay and Leslie Cox look at the changing nature of *Gayspeak*, and both Wouter Geurtsen and Jon Binnie consider the meaning and place of the sadomasochist within the 'gay scene'. Jon Binnie also ponders the meaning and place of the academic researcher in 'studying' his home in the twilight zone.

The book concentrates on these stories as told by gay or bisexual men, not to exclude lesbians, but because we did not have the authority to speak on their behalf. I hope someone else will do that job, because it needs doing.

Part I: It's queer up north

Like all large cosmopolitan conurbations, as a city, Manchester has acquired its own urban history, myths and legends. Titles acquired in its history include "Cottonopolis" and the "Rainy City". It is the home of two great football teams, world class speedway and one of the most enduring first class cricket teams. It is the model for "Weatherfield" the fictitious home of Coronation Street (the opening credits show Manchester terraced housing with blocks of flats crudely superimposed). To many who don't live in Manchester its pervading image is still one cobbled together from Lowry prints and Rita Fairclough's life story: images of men in flat caps with whippets and women with their arms crossed over their pinnies as they gossip in front of their terraced houses.

For those who strive to be aware that Manchester is entering the Twenty First century as one of the world's new metropolises rather than as a mere shadow of its Victorian self, there have been recent opportunities to obtain a revised consciousness of the city's characterization. In the late 1980's "Madchester" emerged. Just as Liverpool in the 1960's was the generator of The Liverpool pop sound so Manchester in the 1980's hatched Joy Division, The Smiths, Stone Roses, New Order and Happy Mondays. The city, for many young people, came to represent "acid house", rave" and ultimately "techno" - all post modern culture booms which captured the youth of the nation's imagination and spending money.

However unknown to most of those who got off the train at Picadilly Station, in the summer of 1992, to go shopping for their baggies, Joe Blogg's flares and a night at the Hacienda, was that they would almost certainly walk within yards of

> one of the fastest growing commercial enterprises in the many faceted and culturally rich night life of the city. [*Pink Guide to Manchester and Salford*, 1991/2]

yet they would not give it a passing glance.

Manchester's lesbian and gay scene would undoubtedly pass them by as they passed by.

Popular images of Manchester are exclusively heterosexual. Unlike those of San Francisco where earthquakes are now inescapably mixed with pink politics, Aids awareness and clone queens, Manchester is supposedly still a city where men are real men, drink Boddingtons/take ecstasy and "their" women love and loathe them, even if that account has moved from the pub to the club. Yet since the early 1980's Manchester has witnessed the development of what is in the United Kingdom, a unique concept. Situated close to the main shopping areas, right in the heart of the city, a 'Gay Village' has flourished.

1 Gay communities and gay space in the city

Paul Hindle

Gay Community

The word 'community' is one of the most over-used and least precise in use in social and geographical literature. At one extreme it can be used to describe a group of people who share a common interest, but who do not usually associate physically or share a territory; for example, a community of scholars. At the other extreme there are highly visible communities of people who live, work, socialise and act politically together; a village is an obvious example. Communities may exist for positive reasons, people wishing to associate for their mutual advantage, or for negative reasons, perhaps to defend themselves against the outside world - here the racial ghetto is the bleakest example.

Gay communities can exist at all levels in this spectrum. In Britain before the 1967 Act, (male) homosexuality was illegal, and the community which existed was only rarely visible to the outside world. It was a private world of contacts, surfacing in only a few pubs and private gay clubs and other places (including public toilets), knowledge of whose existence was passed on by word of mouth. At the other extreme is the oft-quoted Castro area of San Deafened, where gays live, work, shop, socialise, and act politically together in an area where they form the majority of the population. The gay communities of most (western) urban centres fall between their extremes. A visible British gay community began to emerge in the 1970s; Weeks noted two complementary tendencies:

> first the gradual merging of the gay movement and the commercial homosexual sub-culture into a new, more open and diverse culture - the 'ghetto is coming out'; secondly, the gradual, conditional integration of homosexuality into the mainstream heterosexual culture. (Weeks, 1977, p 222)

7

Implicit in this is the argument about whether gay communities should be separate from, or integrated into the rest of society.

Whether or not any sort of gay community comes into existence at all is determined by the number of gay people in an area. There is a continuing controversy over the percentage of gay people in the population as a whole, with different studies using different methods, different definitions, and, not surprisingly, arriving at different results. Gonsoriek and Weinrick (1991) estimate that between 4 and 17% of the population are homosexually orientated (note that they use orientation rather than preference), whilst the more recent (British) National Survey of Sexual Attitudes and Lifestyles (Johnson et al, 1992) give a variety of figures from 6.1% (for any homosexual experience between men) down to 1.1% (for at least one male homosexual partner in the past year). But taking the figures for Greater London, the percentages were between 11.9% and 3.5% respectively; that is, between two and three times greater. This strongly suggest that gay people move to London (and to other cities), for both push and pull reasons: (they may think that 'every street is paved with gays'?), with the net result that the percentage of gays in the population is not the same across the country.

However, these low percentages have been questioned (Tatchell, 1993); the basic statistical point is that the figure of 1.1% represents less that a hundred people out of a sample of just over 8,000. There is also the simple fact that, however good the interviewers might be, there must be a reluctance to admit to any degree of homosexuality in the era of AIDS to a survey which began its life as an official government one.

It is clear, however, that gay communities are overwhelmingly urban, and the size of a gay community is largely determined by the size of an urban area. David Bell underlined the urban nature of gay geographies by subtitling three sections of his 1991 article as "Tales of the city", "More tales of the city", and "Further tales of the city" after Maupin's fictional series documenting gay life in San Francisco. American research has suggested a minimum population of 50,000 is needed to support one gay bar (Harry, 1974), because only a sub-group of gays are sufficiently 'out' to visit a known gay bar. A more recent study of England and Wales showed that, on average, 50,000 men over 20 were required to support a male or 'mixed' gay venue (Hindle, 1992).

In general, the larger the urban area, the greater the number of gay facilities. But the relationship is complicated in several ways. For example, in the age of the private car, lesbians and gay men seem prepared to travel greater distances to visit a particular pub or club. There are also gay resorts, notably Bournemouth, Brighton and Blackpool, which have far more gay facilities (in particular, hotels) than their own populations would support.

Given the polyfocal structure of many British towns, it would be meaningless to try to give a population level at which a town would normally have a gay venue (ie: it is meaningless to try to separate out Camden from London, or Bolton from Manchester). In 1981, Nocton noted that the largest towns without a gay venue were either close of part of larger agglomerations (eg: Dudley, Walsall, Stockton, Basildon, Poole and Birkenhead), or were new towns (eg: Milton Keynes and Telford); his 'odd-one-out' with no gay venue at that time was Norwich.

It is clear that there are remarkably few gay venues in total (around 350 in England and Wales); most gays have to travel a long way to reach a gay venue, even if they live in, say, Greater London or Greater Manchester. It is simply not possible for the vast majority of gays to pop up the road to the 'local gay pub'; it just doesn't exist in most places.

Gays are a typical minority group, held in low esteem by other sections of society, treated differently, and sometimes persecuted. Herek sums this up as "stigma, prejudice and violence" (1991), whilst Boal (1976) lists the functions of an urban minority groups as avoidance, defence, preservation and attack. Knopp notes that

> In Britain today homosexuality is widely considered a threat to family stability, one of the building blocks of 1980s culture. (Knopp, 1990, p 24)

However, gays are an extremely diverse group politically, economically, socially, and often divided by gender, yet they have one very strong common bond. As a result many gays feel bound together in a community, even if it does not always have a physical presence. Bristow takes a very negative view:

> In Britain it is possible to be gay (only) in specific places and spaces: notably, the club scene and social networks often organised around campaigning organisations (phone-lines, fund-raising and so on). However there is no gay 'community' as such. (Bristow, 1989, p 79)

This is probably true of the situation in smaller towns, but must be less true of the gay scene in London, or Manchester's Gay Village where pubs, clubs, shops, and probably residences are located in close proximity to each other.

There are three main strands to a community; the first is simply being visible (gay places, residential areas, businesses, services run by and for gay people), the second is having activities, and the third is being organised socially, financially and politically (Alder & Brenner, 1992). Because of the hidden nature of homosexuality, it is clear that a homosexual community does exist, but it is often not linked to a physical territory:

> a community is an idea as well as a group of people. Those who form a community have a sense of togetherness, of belonging.... (Weightman, 1981, p 107)

So what are the components of a gay community? Fundamentally it is composed of lesbians and gay men (sometimes together, more often quite separate), plus bisexuals, and any 'hangers-on' such as friends and acquaintances. This chapter concentrates on gay men in the city, as lesbians tend to meet and operate socially via interpersonal networks rather than by creating and using territories (Valentine, 1993).

> Although male homosexuals...may have 'come out', not just as individuals but as a community,....their female counterparts remain closeted. (Winchester & White, 1988, p 49)

Nevertheless, some gay women do form part of a city's gay space.
  Within the gay community, perhaps the most important distinction is between those who are 'out' (at home, at work, and/or at play), and those who are 'in the closet', perhaps barely accepting their own sexuality. The latter may only feel part of a gay community by reading *Gay Times* in the privacy of their own home. Indeed, newspapers such as *Gay Times* are a vital part of the development of a gay community. Any notion of community in a physical sense is going to rely on those who are 'out', who are willing to be visible, whether visiting pubs and clubs occasionally, or, ultimately, living and organising in a predominantly gay area. Thus Jackson points out that

> What usually passes for the 'gay community' is actually a minority of the minority - its most politicized and vocal fraction. (Jackson, 1989, p 128)

Harry Britt, a gay political leader in San Francisco, has even argued that

> When gays are spatially scattered, they are not gay, because they are invisible. (quoted in Castells, 1983, p 138)

A further problem is that the most visible gays tend to be white middle-class men, and the published research reflects this.

Perhaps the simplest conclusion is that there are numerous overlapping gay communities, rather than just a single community. And many of these communities have a spatial component.

Gay Space

Gay Space is the physical manifestation of gay community; it can include any area which gays use, a place were gay people can be 'out', and it can exist at a variety of scales from individual premises to agglomerations of those places, and the spaces between them. As such premises tend to be clustered close to the centre of cities, gay areas may emerge, such as Manchester's so-called Gay Village (see below).

> Gay neighbourhoods increasingly play the dual roles of (1) places to which young gay men from the hinterland escape in order to 'come out' or come to terms with their sexuality and (2) bases of community economic and political development. (Lauria & Knopp, 1986, p 161)

The commonest elements of gay space in British towns are pubs, clubs and discos.

> Walking into a gay bar is a momentous act in the life history of a homosexual, because in many cases it is the first time he publicly identifies himself as a homosexual. Of equal importance is the fact that it brings home to him the realization that there are many other young men like himself and, thus, that he is a member of a community and not the isolate he had previously felt himself to be. (Hoffman, 1968, p 16)

Gay bars have probably had more attention from researchers than any other aspect of the gay community; they provide the simplest safe social meeting place. They have even been described as 'colossal closets' (Sage, 1979): they have been and still can be gay ghettos for those gays who feel that they can only safely be 'out' in such places. They are probably the most important single feature of a gay community. Being usually the most visible feature of gay activities in cities, their distribution has been mapped for many cities. Such maps should be used with care, as many venues are transient features, here today and closed tomorrow. Once such establishments were rare, and knowledge of them was passed by word of mouth or reputation; now they are exhaustively and openly listed in the gay press.

The boundaries between pubs, clubs and discos are becoming less clear. More important, the old term 'mixed' for a venue is also changing.

> Back in the good old days you knew who you were. And you knew where to go to.... In you leisure hours, you wanted to escape to the *gay ghetto* where you could be yourself and not feel threatened. (Short, 1993)

Many venues now deliberately set out to attract gay and straight, men and women. Of the 23 venues in Manchester in mid-1993, 5 were described in *Gay Times* as 'mixed'', certainly an underestimate:

> We're talking queer or we're talking integration here. (Short, 1993)

Other venues deliberately aim for a specific section of the market, not just men or women only, but leather, queer, cruisy, short haircut, drag, or SM.

Of course, most towns do not have the variety of pubs and clubs that is be to found in London and Manchester. Many towns of considerable size have only one venue, and many parts of Britain are very remote from any gay venue. But it is clear that many lesbians and gay men simply migrate to one of the larger urban areas so that they can avail themselves to the gay scene.

Gay pubs and clubs can have an enormous economic impact on an area, though it is difficult to quantify. Nevertheless, the 'pink pound' is being spent well into the small hours, providing employment and profit, often in what might otherwise be down-at-heel inner city areas. These gay areas are probably in British inner cities because they were established there in the years after the 1967 Act, when car ownership levels were lower, and night bus services still existed to take the revellers home. There does often seem to be a close proximity of gay venues to bus and coach stations. Cheap premises are also available. Once established in the inner city, inertia has ensured that the gay venues stay there.

The limited number of 'out' gay businesses in most British towns is completely dwarfed by the number in London. Adverts in *Gay Times* reveal that London can offer gay solicitors, accountants, financial advisors, builders, decorators, carpenters, electricians, HIV testing, body piercing and jewellery, telephone dating, massage, escorts, counselling and therapy, shops selling general 'gay goods', leather/rubber goods, sports clothes, books, bikes, videos, travel, as well as pubs, clubs, hotels and health clubs. All these are openly touting for their share of the pink pound; and, through their advertising in the gay press, many are also providing a national service. Of course the total number of gay-owned and/or run businesses is far greater than those which openly advertise themselves as gay.

In Britain open gay involvement in political and cultural life is extremely limited, apart from a few groups with political agendas. There are gay groups attached to the main political parties, others which are independent of them, whilst others seek to help particular groups (eg: disabled, lesbians with children), or work towards other ends (eg: conservation, housing, AIDS). Such groups operate in premises which may form a temporary or permanent part of the gay community's space; they obviously also have a social function. The situation is very different from that in America as described by Lauria and Knopp:

> Gays have done more with space than simply use if as a base for political power. They continually transform and use it is such a way as to reflect gay cultural values and serve the special needs of individual gays vis-a-vis society at large. (1985, p 159)

When we try to look for gay residential areas, gay space suddenly becomes much less visible. If many gays are happy to be seen in pubs, clubs, shops and social groups, they are not keen to be visible at home, as most do not live in gay neighbourhoods, but have to live alongside straight neighbours, many of whom might not be all that keen *if they knew!* Recognisable gay residential areas like those which are reported in so many of the larger American cities are yet to appear in the British townscape. But this is not to say that they do not exist, or are not already in the process of appearing.

Most housing is designed, built, financed and intended for traditional nuclear families. Much of the housing stock is the wrong size for single occupation, and mortgage lenders are not always sympathetic to gays, especially to gay women. Single men are often in a better position, having higher disposable income levels, but they can have difficulty obtaining endowment mortgages due to fears about AIDS.

Many open spaces such as streets, squares and parks, have their gay areas, used for recreation or cruising, but for legal reasons they are rarely listed. Rarely mentioned in polite company are the 'tearooms' (ie: public toilets - referred to in the United Kingdom as 'cottages'), described by Laud Humphreys (1972) in which much covert sexual activity certainly goes on, though this usually anonymous activity can be viewed as the ultimate failure of any notion of gay community.

One possible end product of the creation of gay space is a segregated 'gay ghetto', similar to ethnic and racial ghettos, but in this case defined by a combination of sexuality, lifestyle and culture. Levine says that

> an urban neighbourhood is a 'gay ghetto' if it possesses....gay institutions in number, a conspicuous and locally dominant gay

13

subculture that is socially isolated from the larger community, and a residential population that is substantially gay (1979, p 185)

A ghetto can be viewed in a much more negative light; an area where gays congregate for safety, a visible sign of the lack of acceptance of homosexuality by the rest of the community. Levine concluded that the Castro area of San Francisco (among others) was then a gay ghetto.

San Francisco as a Model

San Francisco undoubtedly has one of the most obvious and powerful 'out' gay communities in the world. In 1980 about 17% of its total population was estimated to be gay, and because of high gay voter registration and turnout, up to 30% of those voting in city election might be gay. It features highly in literature, to the extent that "one might be forgiven for thinking... all gay men congregate in San Fransisco..." (Bell, 1991, p 323). But what has happened in San Francisco has also happened in most large American cities.

The population was first described and analysed in depth (as a piece of social geography) in Manuel Castells' *The City and the Grassroots* (1983). Despite this seminal work, the topic has been largely or totally ignored by many subsequent textbooks; the most recent text (entitled: *Communities within Cities*) mentions gay communities very briefly, twice, both times as an example of a 'lifestyle community', first linked with orthodox Jews, and second with Bagwan Rajneesh (Davies & Herbert, 1995, ps 2, 53)! One of the rare exceptions to this rule is Peter Jackson's *Maps of Meaning* (1989), where gender *and sexuality* are given a chapter to themselves.

In seeking to delimit the classic gay territory in San Francisco, Castells drew on five types of information; gay bars and other social gathering places, gay businesses, voting patterns for Harvey Milk (a gay candidate, later murdered), multiple male households from voter lists, and crucially, "key informants" (pollsters in gay electoral campaigns) who would have a down-to-earth knowledge of the area. He was able to show how the gay areas had developed since the 1960s.

The first San Francisco gay area emerged in the 1940s in the Tenderloin district, adjacent to downtown (Figure 1).

There were networks, but no community places, but no territory. (Castells, 1983, p 154)

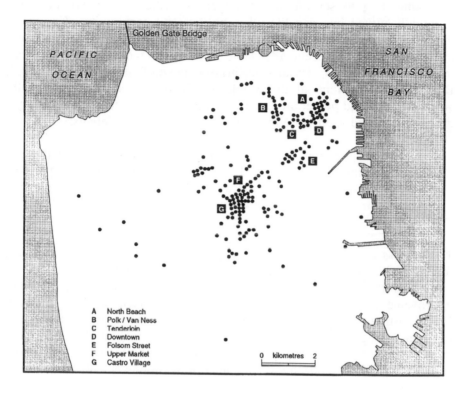

Gay Businesses in San Francisco, 1979
(after Castells)

During the 50s and 60s the network expanded and gay bars appeared around Polk and Van Ness; a gay residential area began to develop here too. But it was the Stonewall Revolt in New York in 1969 that started a new era, with gays migrating to several of the larger US cities. The gay networks eventually turned into gay lifestyles, politics and community. Gays took over the Castro area; it was being vacated by the Irish working class, and provided plenty of decent affordable housing to rent, suitable for non-traditional households. Usually, businesses moved first, and bars followed. But at the same time in the South of Market areas a less politically concerned gay and poorer area was growing, whilst yet another, richer, gay group established itself close to the elite area of Pacific Heights:

> What is clear from San Francisco is that the evaluation of the gay areas is complex, and is tied in with a host of social and political factors. ...the building of the Castro ghetto was inseparable from the development of the gay community as a social movement. (Castells, p 157)

The process was regarded by many as part of gay liberation and gay pride; for them, the gay areas had been literally been 'liberated'.

An important side effect on the city was the impact on housing; improvement and gentrification began among the Victorian houses of the Castro district in particular in the 1970's. One reason for this is that many gay men (though by no means all) having no traditional families, had more money to spend. Others organised themselves in alternative household structures (such as collectives) and undertook improvements themselves. Knopp notes that:

> Housing renovation... is a powerful vehicle for gay cultural expression. Furthermore, the concentrations of gay people in these neighbourhoods provide a measure of protection against discrimination and a territorial basis for the development of community resources and power. (1990, p 25)

A negative effect was that gays put pressure on poor areas alongside (notably the Black/Latino Mission area), as affluent white gay men started to guy houses, forcing poorer tenants out.

These movements of population constitute part of the restructuring of the city; its internal economic, social, cultural, political and sexual geographies have changed dramatically in the last forty years. This 'urban renaissance' is now a widespread phenomenon, and some of its potential implications were spotted by Edmund White on his travels in gay America:

One can foresee in the near future an era when the big old American cities... will be populated by an elite made up of the affluent young, the wealthy retired, rich foreigners and middle-class, childless couples - and gays. (1980, p 61)

An academic approach to the same issue can be found in Lauria & Knopp who argue that:

Gays, in essence, have seized an opportunity to combat oppression by creating neighbourhoods over which they have maximum control and which meet long-neglected needs. (1986, p 161)

Gay Space in Manchester

Many of Manchester's gay spaces are remarkably concentrated in its 'Gay Village' (Figure 2). The Gay Village is extremely well defined on the map; Bloom Street used to be its spine, but this is now being supplemented by the recently pedestrianised Canal Street. Fifteen gay premises are all within 150 metres of each other, but this relatively small area is important in community terms. To quote Adler and Brenner (1992, p 31) more fully: a gay neighbourhood needs (amongst other things):

community activity - fairs, block parties, street celebrations etc., some kind of public, collective affirmation of the people who live in the neighbourhood, even if it is only strolling out in the evening.

Manchester's Gay Village provides that space and activities go on, even if most of the participants are not residents of the area itself.

The simple fact that a Gay Village is recognised in Manchester establishes a territory in which gays may feel at home, or safer then elsewhere in the city. But it could also become a ghetto, an area where gays could become isolated and segregated. It is perhaps better seen in a more positive light as an area created by, or even liberated by gays.

The Village is a relatively recent phenomenon, and the social scene was the first element to develop. The Rembrandt is always quoted as Manchester's oldest gay pub, going back to pre-war days when it had a different name. In the 1960s coffee bar era there were meeting places for those in the know around the top of Oxford Street. But it was the 1967 Sexual Offences Act which allowed gay venues to operate more openly and in greater numbers, and by the mid-1970s the Village area already had four pubs surrounding a club (Napoleon's); though there was a clutch of bars and clubs in the area

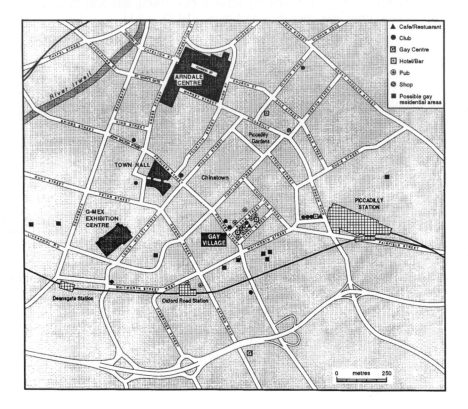

Manchester's Gay Village, 1993

between the Town Hall and Deansgate. Since then the total number of gay premises has trebled, and the concentration in the Village has intensified.

In this core area in 1993, little large than a single block, there are seven pubs/bars, a hotel/bar, three clubs, two cafes, and two shops. In addition there is a gay medical practice, taxi service, and a hairdressers. All the gay premises lie within a few minutes walk. The Village area, once full of run-down cotton wholesaling premises, has now been much improved, notably by the improvement and pedestrianisation of Canal Street, alongside the Rochdale Canal. This initiative was driven by the Central Manchester Development Corporation (CMDV) as part of its overall scheme to revitalise the 'zone of discard' around the city's Central Business District. Curiously, the Gay Village lies immediately next door to another urban village, the even more recently developed Chinatown.

Manchester's gay social scene is the largest outside London. It attracts visitors from a large catchment area, even to the extent that some gays come to Manchester for a holiday. The variety of venues is great. First there are about a dozen pubs and bars which are open for the usual pub hours, most are mixed to a greater or lesser extent, but each has its own character; one has cabaret, another has a gallery, two have nightclubs after hours, and three are also hotels. Several might be described as fringe venues, sometimes in the lists, sometimes not, used by gays, but not part of the core of gay pubs. Changing landlords can cause pubs to drop in and out of the lists; a new landlord might not want to attract the gay pounds (and the reputation which goes with them).

The dozen clubs/discos/dance clubs are equally diverse; there are traditional clubs, whilst others aim to be trendy or cruisy. Most are geared for gay men, some are 'mixed', and one is principally for women. Two give space for the leather/rubber trade, others are described as 'rave' or 'queer'. Some are small, others enormous, most run until 2 am, one until 4 am, and one until 6 am. Most operate throughout the week, several open only four nights, two operate one night a week, and one operates only once a month. in order to try to get as much trade as possible, clubs often close for refurbishment, which can mean a new name. A 1993 issue of *Gay Times* gave the same club twice under different names. On the other hand, some of the more traditional clubs have been fixtures for many years. They tend to operate in cheap premises (often in basements), and this area has a reasonable supply of such premises.

Compared to London, the list of gay businesses (other than the pubs and clubs) in Manchester is small; solicitors advertising in the gay community (who are not all gay themselves), a 'gay goods' shop, a radical bookshop which has a gay section, two taxi firms (one for women), and then a motley list including counselling, therapy, photography, escorts, massage and telephone chat lines and dating.

The history of gay politics in Manchester probably has two major events. The first was the formation of the North-Western Committee for Homosexual Law Reform in the 1960s, which later became the Campaign for homosexual Equality; CHE had its first headquarters in Manchester. The second event was the change of policy by Manchester City Council in 1983 when a radical section of the Labour Party gained control. It implemented a general policy of equality opportunities throughout all its activities, of which its attitudes to gay men and women formed a part. It was thus no accident that the massive national rally protesting about the Conservative government's Clause 28 (making it illegal for Councils to 'promote homosexuality') was held in Manchester in 1988.

The gay community had started its own Gay Centre in the 1970's, running phonelines and offering counselling; the Council rehoused the Centre in new purpose built premises in the 1980's. It has a wide remit to serve the gay and lesbian communities, though it is unfortunate some distance from the Gay Village. It operates at the political level as well as the social. The Gay Centre has only one full-time paid officer, and has to rely on over 90 volunteers, most of whom staff the various phonelines, notably Gay Switchboard, which currently receives some 20,000 calls each year. Gay Switchboards provide a vital service, especially for newcomers to the scene, giving advice and help as well as information.

The Council has appointed a Gay Liaison Officer in its Equal Opportunities section at the Town Hall, paid by the City Council, whose job is to both develop and implement policies put to and agreed by the Council's Equal Opportunities Committee. The Council had until recently Gay Mens' and Lesbians' Sub-Committees, and though these have been disbanded, the Council still maintains a commitment to consult the gay community.

Most recently a Lesbian and Police Issues Group has been established, including a Police Inspector from the Greater Manchester Constabulary. This is perhaps the most outgoing campaigning group currently operating in Manchester, and its very existence is all the more surprising after the years when the police force was led by the virulently homophobic Chief Constable James Anderton, who (amongst other bizarre acts) once tried to close a gay club by using an archaic Act forbidding 'licentious dancing'.

An unusual move has been the creation of the Village Charity, run by local businessmen, designed to raise funds for people in the North West living with HIV and AIDS. Its physical presence is seen for three days each August Bank Holiday when a carnival fills the streets of the Gay Village. *Gay Times* also listed 28 special interest groups, including alcoholic, conservation, disabled, religious, political, AIDS, occupational, naturist, parents, leather, housing, deaf, student and youth groups; many of these are more social than political.

A separate gay cultural life is barely visible, though Manchester is highly rated as a cultural centre, despite its size. The Contact Theatre Company is noted for its links with the gay community, there is a gay theatre group, and the Cornerhouse cinema complex attracts a mixed clientele. However, Manchester has hosted the first two National Festivals of Lesbian and Gay Arts, under the heading 'It's Queer Up North'.

Observing where gays live is very difficult, as Castells noted in San Francisco. There are areas with comparable housing stock (including old houses in reasonable condition, ripe for renovation, available for rent) between the inner city and the suburbs, then there are such identifiable places; in London, Camden and Earl's Court certainly have a high percentage of gay residents (mirrored by the location of gay venues).

But in Manchester gay living areas are not so obvious; anecdotal evidence suggests that there is a corridor running south from the city centre, different parts of which attract different gay residents. It has been clear for some time that Chorlton-cum-Hardy and Whalley Range (2-3 miles from the City Centre) are 'friendly' or 'liberal' suburban areas where wealthier middle-class gays with more disposable income prefer to live, though there are no gay facilities in these areas. There is virtually no Council housing in these areas, the housing mix being roughly 60% owner-occupied and just under 40% private rented (these figures and those in the next two paragraphs are ward level data from the 1991 Census).

Closer to the centre there are areas where difficult-to-let council flats predominate, notably the infamous Hulme area only a mile from the City Centre; here 90% of the housing stock is Council rented, and 84% are flats. These flats are particular unattractive to families with children, and consequently are let to single people or groups of singles; clearly this group is likely to include gay men and women. Letting certain areas to gay people is however not a Council policy. The net result is that 50% of households in Hulme has only one resident (compared to the City's overall figure of 34%). Further anecdotal evidence reports that one block of flats not too far from the city centre (which has a high proportion of gay men) is known to its residents as 'Fairy Towers'.

But an important housing trend of the past few years in Britain has been the regeneration of inner city areas. In Manchester, old offices and warehouses have been turned into flats, elsewhere whole new estates have been built, all close to the city centre, where, of course, the Gay Village is also to be found. Much of this property is owner-occupied (for example, Grandby House), whilst a smaller percentage is available for rent from housing associations (such as India House). It is certain that some gay men have moved into such eminently suitable accommodation; proving it is a different matter! The 1991 Census shows that 47% of households in Central Ward as a whole have a single resident.

Another way to try to see where gay men live is to scan the electoral registers looking for single and double male households; the method is obviously rather crude, and the results should be treated with care. However, a survey of over 450 households in nine sets of recently developed flats and estates in Manchester's Central Ward revealed that 44% appeared to be occupied by single males, 5% by two males (with different surnames), while the composition of a further 11% was unclear (usually because only initials were given in the register). Thus it appears that not only are gays migrating to cities, but they are moving within cities to particular areas.

If there are areas where gays tend to live, there are others where they do not; certain areas of the city are strongly homophobic (Moston is often cited as such), and it would be difficult if not dangerous for any openly gay person or couple to live in such areas. A brief survey of the electoral register for Moston showed single male households to be extremely rare (less than 5%); and judging by their old-fashioned first names, it would be a shrewd guess that most of these few are widowers.

In Manchester there is clearly emerging gay residential areas, but their small size and lack of concentration means that there is, as yet, no gay vote in any one of the city wards.

Conclusion

Are they any lessons of the San Francisco experience for British cities? Winchester and White may be going to far when they suggest that

> The high-profile gay male community, with its very visible influence on functional space in the city, is possibly only fully apparent in San Francisco. (1988, p 49)

Manchester is the only British city with a concentrated gay area (though London is now attempting to copy it, following the old adage "What Manchester does today, London does tomorrow"), and Manchester's place in the urban hierarchy is not dissimilar to that of San Francisco.

Overall, San Francisco probably has little to tell us about how Manchester's gay community might develop. It is clear that the same social and political driving forces are not present; Britain in the 1990's is hardly comparable to San Francisco in the 1970's. The formative factors, the scale and the time are all different. Writing in general terms, Bell came to the same conclusion:

> ...... researchers should be aware that findings are not fully transferable across space, time, gender, lifestyle. The 'gay community' must thus be seen in its full diversity ... there are different gay geographies of living, working and relaxing. (Bell, 1991, p 328)

Manchester's gay area is still without a clearly visible residential component, principally because there is a lack of cheap accommodation for rent close to the village. There are Council flats for rent, but they are a mile or so away, and there are the newly refurbished inner city flats, but these are more expensive.

What is the future of gay space in the British city? Winchester and White (1988) suggest that the controlling factors for the location of marginalised groups are wealth, power, social acceptability, and legality.

First, the changing job market in the city centre and inner city areas (towards service industries) may attract a high proportion of gay people not only to work, but also to live in these areas. There is often a disincentive for them to live in heterosexist and even homophobic family neighbourhoods elsewhere in the city. But the appropriate housing stock has to be available. Thus whether gay villages will develop more generally probably depends on the availability of suitable housing; Manchester is not well provided in this respect, but other smaller cities do have potential for development.

Second, if such villages develop, will they be ghettos, or integrated with the rest of the community? Third, it remains to be seen if the gay vote will ever have an impact here, as it has in Castro and West Hollywood. Political power can clearly have a great impact on the development of gay community and gay space. Fourth, the impact of AIDS is difficult to forecast; it is widely recognised that the actions of the gay community has reduced the transmission of HIV. However the deaths may be offset by the seemingly ever-increasing number of those who come out and identify themselves as gay.

It remains to be seen whether Manchester's Gay Village will be the model for the developments of gay communities and gay space in Britain.

Acknowledgements

The author is grateful to Terry Waller, Gay Liaison Officer at Manchester City Council and to Rob Pennock, the full-time worker at the Gay Centre for giving up time to talk over the various issues.

Bibliography

Adler, S. & Brenner, J., (1992) "Gender and space: lesbians and gay men in the city", *International Journal of Urban and Regional Research* 16/1, pp 24-34.

Bell, D.J., (1991) "Insignificant others: lesbian and gay geographies", *Area* 23/4, pp 323-329.

Boal, F.W., (1976) "Ethnic residential segregation", Herbert, D.T. & Johnston R.J. (eds) *Spatial Processes and Form* Vol 1, Wiley, London.

Bristow, J. (1989) "Being gay: politics, identity, pleasure.", *New Formations* 9, pp 61-81.

Castells, M., (1983) *The City and the Grassroots*, Edwards Arnold, London.

Davies, V.K.D & Herbert, D.T., (1983) *Communities Within Cities*, Belhaven Press, London.

Gonsoriek, J.C. & Weinrich, J.D., (1991) "The definition and scope of sexual orientation", Gonsoriek, J.C. & Weinrick, J.D., (eds) *Homosexuality: research implications for public policy* pp 1-12.

Harry, J., (1974) "Urbanisation and the Gay Life", *Journal of Sex Research*, 10/3, pp 238-247.

Herek, G. M., (1991) "Stigma, prejudice, and violence against lesbians and gay men", Gonsoriek, J. C., & Weinrich, J. D., (eds) *Homosexuality: research implications for public policy* pp 60-80.

Hindle, B. P., (1992) *Gay Space: contact and community* Paper presented to Sexuality and Space Network Conference, London.

Hoffman, M., (1968) *The Gay World: male homosexuality and the social creation of evil.*

Humphreys, L., (1972) *Out of the Closets: the sociology of homosexual liberation*, Prentice-Hall, New Jersey.

Jackson, P., (1989) *Maps of Meaning: an introduction to cultural geography*, Unwin Hyman, London.

Johnson, A. M., Wadsworth, J., Wellings, K., Bradshaw, S., and Field, J., (1992) "Sexual lifestyles and HIV risk", *Nature*, 360 No 6403, 3rd December, pp 410-412.

Knopp, L. M., (1990) "Social consequences of homosexuality", *Geographical Magazine* May, pp 20-25.

Lauria, M. and Knopp, L., (1985) "Towards an analysis of the role of the gay communities in the urban renaissance", *Urban Geography*, 6/2, pp 152-169.

Levine, M. P., (1979) "Gay Ghetto", Levine,M.P. (ed) *Gay Man: the sociology of male homosexuality*, pp 182-204.

Nocton, C. W., (1983) *Gay Space: a geographical study with special reference to England and Wales*, Unpublished dissertation, Department of Geography, University of Salford.

Sage, W., (1979) "Inside the Colossal Closet", Levine, M.P. (ed) *Gay Men: the sociology of male homosexuality*, pp 148-163.

Short, B., (1993) "Myths and mixtures in Manchester", *Gay Times* 178 (July, 1993) pp 50-51.

Tatchell, P., (1993) "Where are the missing millions?" *Gay Times* 172 (January 1993) pp 14-15.

Valentine, G., (1993) "Desparately seeking Susan: a geography of lesbian friendships" *Area* 25/2, pp 109-116.

Weeks, J., (1977) *Coming Out: homosexuality politics in Britain*, Quartet Books, London.

Weightman, B. A., (1981) "Towards a Geography of the Gay Community", *Journal of Cultural Geography* , 1, pp 106-112.

White, E., (1980) *States of Desire: Travels in Gay America*, Andre Deutsch, London.

Winchester, H. P. M. & White, P. E., (1988) "The location of marginalised groups in the inner city", *Environment and Planning D: Society and Space*, 6/1, pp 37/54.

2 Consuming differences: The collaboration of the gay body with the cultural state

Stephen Whittle

Saying What We Mean

In the following paper, the word 'QUEER' is used as Lisa Duggan does (in her article in Summer 1992's Socialist Review) to enable the lesbian and gay social scene to be discussed in such a way as to include other lifestyles whose icons are heavily associated by cultural outsiders with the culture of gay life, politics, and practices. This particular English use of "queer" enables there to be the notion of a 'Queer' community, that is a collectivity no longer defined solely by the gender of its members sexual partners but its unity is that of a shared dissent from the dominant organisation of sex and gender. In this way sexualities that are different from lesbian and gay sexualities but which have associated cultural features are discussed through references to the commonness they appear to have, to those who don't have a lesbian or gay sexuality. Thus those people who use the facilities of Manchester's Gay scene, who are not lesbian or gay and yet who are not straight, are placed in some form of unity by outsiders. This usage of 'queer' has many critics, but I wish to use it to signify the view from outside, and not the view from inside Manchester's lesbian and gay community.

Queer Nights

> The whole fabric of personal life is imprinted with colours from
> elsewhere. Not to acknowledge this and to pretend the private
> is free leads to false analysis. (K.O'Donovan in *Sexual Divisions
> in Law*, 1985)

Living in a city, does not necessarily mean having the same experience of urban life as other city dwellers. When seminars were taking place in the Manchester Institute for Popular Culture, about the social and cultural influences in the night time economy of Manchester, some of us involved found ourselves hearing the names of clubs and bars that as individuals we had sometimes heard of, but had never visited.

Yet, we were people who had actively participated in the city's night life, in one case for over 20 years. But it became apparent that our understanding of the city at night, was not the same as that of the majority of Institute members. It was very different. Our knowledge of Manchester at night was situationally distinct, historically distinct even imaginatively distinct. Where we went at night, what we remembered of those evenings and why we went out were a different story. Within our individual stories we had differing plots, but there were certain similarities in each other's tales. It became obvious that we had been living in a different city from that of our fellows. As a result we had a different paradigm and discourse of the city's night time economy.

The Institute were discussing clubs and bars that were outside of our social life, that we had never accessed - because they were not clubs for people like us - 'queer people'. As such some of us wished to include *our discourse* in with *the wider discourse* of Manchester's night time city. To that extent I searched for the history of Manchester's Gay Village from oral, ephemeral and formal sources and it is that which makes up the central part of this essay.

Firstly though I wanted a theoretical framework which could accommodate my roles both as a geographer and a lawyer. The question of 'policing space' became central to this after my first few informal interviews with people who used the 'gay scene' in Manchester. My initial interviewees often mentioned policing as an area of importance to them. Currently it was a lack of policing that was of concern. Very few had had any bad experiences of the police, but they felt that there had never been a police presence on the streets to protect the rights of lesbians and gay men. Since the development of a Gay Village area in Manchester, they argued for the provision of protection to be provided for the potentially very vulnerable users of what was now a concentrated site. An area which could be easily targeted either by 'queer bashers', or by the police in order to protect, if they chose to do so. My framework became: with the redevelopment and official acknowledgement of Manchester's Gay Village, has Gay Liberation really come to town? Can the Gay Village really and truly become gay space which is welcoming and safe for its users?

Manchester's gay nightlife has since the mid 1950's, provided a backdrop to the ongoing battle between the state's interests (as embodied in the Greater Manchester Police Force) and lesbians and gay men. I have looked at this with an awareness of two differing views of the political and social contests that have occurred in order to gain the physical and social space now known as Manchester's Gay Village.

The first; that the Gay Village is symbolic of the post-modern acknowledgement of alternative lifestyles with their varying truths. We have learnt in our cities to live together, in such a way that we do not as such affect or judge each others choices, in particular as far as sexual habits are concerned. Tolerance has become part of the way in which a society gains lawfulness. Lawfulness is a state of being in which the fullness of law permeates us and we acknowledge the appropriateness, the correctness of being at one with the law. Alternative lifestyles do not have to be condemned because they no longer take a problematic form, they are no longer at odds with (on the edges of) the state but are welcomed into the centre. They become part of its richness, and contribute towards both the state's economic well being and that of the individual. This view will be enlarged using a Gramscian perspective of hegemonic control.

The second view is one in which Gay lifestyles have always been marginalised. From being outside of the law, they move to being within the law, but not part of the law. This has been achieved not through a romantic notion of tolerance but by the marginalised group kicking so hard that eventually the walls of the citadel have crumbled - at least in one section. As a group moves into the centre it is not tolerated - it is merely not expelled. Acceptance does not necessarily mean understanding, it can mean that the grief and expense of expulsion, which is seen as the only alternative to acceptance, is reckoned to be too high (at least at this moment in time). In this version, Manchester's Gay Village is a hard won bastion of gay rights situated within, yet at the same time without, the bastion of the state. It is a space that has been physically gained but not morally realised. It remains on the edge of our consciousness, though it may be at the heart of our city.

A Gramscian Perspective

The state must maintain the relations on which it depends ie. the existing social order, as Gramsci put it:

> the most reasonable and concrete thing that can be said about the ethical and cultural state is this: every state is ethical in as much as one of its most important functions is to raise the great mass of the population to a particular cultural and moral level, a level (or type) which corresponds to the needs of the productive forces of development, and hence to the interests of the ruling classes. (Gramsci, SPN, 258-9 [Q8 para179], in Forgacs (ed) 1988, p 234)

Anything that threatens that must be controlled or neutralised. Gramsci drew attention to the aspects of class rule that are non-violent (whereas previous marxists regarded the state largely as the organised violence of the ruling class). Ultimately the ruling class retains power because of its control of the police and armed forces, but it is through "civil" society that the ruling classes guarantee their long term control.

Hegemony is the identification by the dominated classes as their own, those interests which belong to the ruling classes. By drawing the dominated classes into an alliance, it is able to exercise its authority seemingly without coercion and by consent. This consent can be won by the ruling classes making concessions or reforms that do not touch or alter its essential interests. The community may face control and coercion in the campaign by the ethical and cultural state. Pressure is applied to the individual in order to obtain collaboration and consent to the state's coercion. In the case of homosexuality, the straight population is pressured to think that queer is the other, outside of justice. But queer people also have to be pressured into participating in the society of collective man. Consent may not be possible, but collaboration may be.

Collaboration can be gained, by the state in various ways. Threats, violence, greed, patriotism are just some of the methods. Consumerism in a capitalist society is also a way, as it is ultimately controlled by the state, which dictates which goods and services can be sold and who shall have the means of barter and how much. The development and growth of Manchester's Gay Village can be viewed as part of this pressure to collaborate.

The alternative presents a view in which Manchester's Gay Village is as a result of a war almost won. After over 300 years of legal oppression, many gay rights have been obtained because of the battles that have taken place on the streets, because of the martyrs and because of the concessions that have been gained from the state and its forces. The Queer Nation has come to town.

Gay Space and Safety

In either scenario, there has been gained 'gay space'. Geographical space in which to be a physical presence, and ethical space in which to *be*. In the Gramscian perspective, the geographical space supports a notion of 'being' which in turn supports the state's interests. As such it is safe space in which 'being gay' is to be welcomed as a contributor to the state's interests through your social and sexual habits (which of course follow the state directed guidelines on safe sex) and your economic means (which as a gay person, without the apparent costs of dependants, contribute towards the gentrification of otherwise run down and unattractive inner city). Space is available in those areas which were otherwise becoming centres and meeting places for dangerous forces which challenged the state's interests and power base. Being gay has moved from being dangerous to being safe, not just for the gay man or lesbian but also for the state.

Alternatively, if we take the view of 'battles fought and won', being gay has not become safe in itself. Gay men and lesbians are still members of the dangerous forces which challenge the state. They again have gained ground, both geographically and ethically, but none of it is safe. The geographical space gained is under constant threat from the forces of the state including the supposedly 'gay' activity of gentrification (a Gramscian notion, in which the oppressed classes identify with the values of their rulers). Gay men are often prime movers in the gentrification of inner city landscapes - is this to make it their own unique space, or is this to make it less unique and more like it belongs to the outside suburban areas?

Either way, the space becomes more accessible and attractive to 'ordinary' heterosexuals, not less, and as such heterosexual society is seen to attempt to reclaim it, buying their way in, through such notions as mixed clubs and bars. In a similar way, we could see a gentrification of the gay body. Being clones rather than queens, is a way of become more like non-gay people. The notion of reclamation still has a place on the site of the body, as the state can now reclaim the (more) acceptable to act as its tools of power - 'you may be gay, but we will let you join the police, army, etc' (another Gramscian notion). In this second perspective, geographical and ethical gay space are in constant danger from the hegemonic forces, because they are viewed as outside dangers which have penetrated the heart.

So who has won the battle, Gramsci's ethical and cultural state, or the Queer Nation? Did the origins of Manchester's Gay village come from gay people to cater for gay people's needs? Or was it a developmental, commercial and policing ploy to keep lesbians and gay men in a separate, easily surveillance, easily exploited, easily commercialised and easily sanitised environment? If achieved, the village could be the acceptable face of gay liberation, whilst portraying the liberal economic world's acceptance and promotion of gay people's rights, and at the same time enable the city's commercial, retail and financial dealers to make a buck or two out of an otherwise under exploited market.

In both perspectives there is, I conclude, an illusion of safe space, and I want to address the issue of safe space in this essay on Manchester's Gay Village.

Safe Space in Manchester ?

In Manchester, the question of whether there really is a safe gay community which welcomes all lesbians and gays and which provides a social life for them in safe space, is taking place at a time when to all appearances a social life is much more easily obtained for lesbians and gays than it ever was. There is apparently much less stigma attached to being lesbian or gay. Manchester's Queer city is now used by and caters for people with many different sexualities from those encountered on the 'straight' scene. It provides a social life and entertainment for those on the straight gay scene. It also hosts the Wednesday evening meetings of the Northern Concorde - one of the biggest straight transvestite clubs in the country, the social events of the SM and leather scene, the gatherings of Transsexuals, the meetings of the Mackintosh Brigade and the clandestine dates of those who use the contact magazines to meet others for 'interesting sex'.

Most of these people meet together in, and use the facilities of what is referred to as the 'Gay Scene' in Manchester. Now in the 1990's there is the 'Gay Village' in Manchester, and queer people can go to many straight clubs, albeit on specific nights and find their entertainment needs catered for. For example the Hacienda (Manchester's most famous night club) at least one night a month is a welcoming space to gay men and lesbians. Also, September 1993 has again seen as part of the Manchester Festival the celebration of Queer sexuality, "It's queer up north" as part of the city's very highly publicised arts and music festival.

It was only with the 1967 Sexual Offences Actthat it became possible to open a bar catering for gay people, as prior to then it would have been an offence. In 1965 the licensee of the Union Pub, situated on the corner of Canal Street and Princess Street, was imprisoned for a year for having "outraged public decency" by "exploiting abnormality". Ironically the publicity this conviction generated enabled the Union to remain, to this day, as one of the most well known gay bars of the city, under its new name "The New Union". For many years it was the bar that young lesbians and gay men would go to as they first dared explore their sexuality, primarily because it was the only gay bar they would have heard of.

Before 1967, there were places around the city where gay men would go to meet other gay men. There were various 'cottages' (public toilets) which were popularly known as cruising areas where men could go to meet other men either for sex in the cottage, or to meet and go elsewhere. There were two main cottages in the centre of Manchester, one was on Bridgewater Street, at its junction with Oxford Street, the other was at Knott Mill at the southern end of Deansgate. Near these sites there were to develop bars where gay men in particular went. On Oxford Street, with its entrance situated just opposite the Bridgewater Street cottage, from the early 60's to the early 70's when it was closed, the Long Bar under the Odeon Cinema was well known as a cruising bar for gay men. Certainly by the time of its closure in 1973, its reputation was as a place where you went to make a pick up for sex. Knott Mill had a slightly more up-market reputation, and it was seen as being somewhere the police did not bother with.

It would seem appropriate that when the 1967 law reforms enabled the first openly gay clubs in the city to open that they would be sited near the main cruising areas. Opened near Knott Mill was a club initially called Rouge, later it became the Queens Club. Sited on Queen Street on the north side of Deansgate, very close to the Bootle Street Police station, there continued the uneasy truce between the club and the police, that there had been between the punters and rent boys and the police just down the street.

The Queens Club was followed by the Rockingham on Brazennose Street, which had originally opened in 1966, gradually changing its image to become an openly gay bar. Later after the Queen's Club had closed it would be some years before Slingsby's bar and Heroes Club were to open just close by on Wood Street. The gay scene was beginning to be recognisable as such, but apart from the Rembrandt and Union Pubs, it was sited between Albert Square and Deansgate, some distance from where the Gay Village now is.

However Deansgate was not to last long as the main gay centre for gay people in Manchester. The first club, rather than bar, to open near to what is now the Gay village was Samantha's which opened on Back Picadilly in 1970. It moved a couple of years later to George Street where as Samantha's II it was between what is now the Gay Village area and the Odeon Long Bar on Oxford Street. At around the same time in 1972, Napoleon's 21 Club opened.

Still open, and now simply called Napoleon's, it is the longest existing gay club in Manchester (perhaps even the longest existing club of any type in the city). It is sited on the corner of Bloom Street and Sackville Street.

Manchester became home, in the early 70's, to one of the collectively largest and most powerful gay liberation movements in Britain. This combined with its massive student population (it has four universities within easy reach of the city centre) meant that many young lesbians and gays were attracted to the city, and the higher education institutions meant that for many they could legitimately leave home and come to live here. They were in turn to provide the clientele and consumers for the development of a gay social life within the city. Not only were they to support gay bars and clubs but also other aspects of lesbian and gay life.

When James Anderton became head of the Greater Manchester Police Force in 1976, homophobic views were to head a policy which would lead to a clampdown by the police of many expressions of lesbian and gay lifestyles. This would lead the clubs and bars, the student gay societies and the gay liberation movement in the city into an uncomfortable alliance against the police.

Napoleons, one of the most reactionary clubs in the city with its a men only door policy, was to find itself at the centre of that uneasy coalition when it became a particular target of police harassment during the late 1970's and the early 1980's.

Dirty Dancing

In 1978 the Police raided Napoleon's. They instituted a prosecution under a 19th century by-law for "licentious dancing". At that time Napoleons had a licence for a Saturday and Sunday night dancing club, and approximately 150 people would use the up stairs dance floor on each of the nights. However it was at that time possible to see through the windows of the club (they have since been shuttered) and in 1978 the News of the World ran a series of articles about how disgraceful it was that men could be seen, dancing together.

The owners of the club defended the prosecution, and there was also an outcry at the time which gained massive support from the University and Polytechnic students (due mostly to the efforts of their respective Gaysocs). Ultimately the prosecution failed, and the by-law was repealed - but the shutters did go up on the windows of the upstairs dance floor.

Not Tonight Anderton

Just after midnight on the 17th November 1984, over twenty (mostly plain clothed) policemen, once again, raided Napoleon's. Customers were asked to provide their names and address, the club membership list was seized, and the club was eventually forcibly closed for the rest of the evening though not until there had been a protest of sorts. In a scene reminiscent of the start of the Stonewall Street riots, about 20 transvestites were in the club that night, and they refused to move. As one gay man put it:

> The police were frightened to go in and move them, they didn't know how to, because they didn't like to touch them - but for some time the police were standing outside wondering whether to go away (interview).

One policeman was heard to say:

We've been trying to close these queer places for years (in *Mancunian Gay*, Dec/Jan 1985, No 38, P 2)

Finally they did manage to close the club for the rest of the night, but the consequences for the police and the gay community were significant.

Fighting Back

In the May 1984 Municipal Elections, the Labour group in Manchester had been re-elected, with the radical left in control for the first time. They were to pursue an equal opportunities policy very rigorously.

The raid on Napoleon's had been an undoubted mistake; the police had either not realised the extent of the lesbian and gay community's opposition to their heavy handed approach, or if it had been intended as a direct challenge to the newly elected radical city council all they did was stiffen the resolve within the council to support the fight for equal opportunities. Either way on January 1st 1985, seven Equal Opportunities Officers were appointed to the council, two of whom were to be responsible for gay issues. Further for the first time club owners found solidarity with their customers. This:

> might not seem so surprising that [they] should be concerned when the Police clamp down on specifically gay establishments but the reality has been that it has taken a fairly serious attack to happen in order for Gay businesses and Gay Rights organisations to get together under the same roof (Lowry. A, *Mancunian Gay*, March 1985, No 40, pp 10-11)

That they could see the commonness of their cause was a great step forward in 1985. This unity between lesbians and gay men, the city council and gay business's could almost be marked as the beginning of the evolution of the Gay Village as an idea.

By 1984 there had been an attempt to revitalise the Deansgate cruising area with the opening of Stuffed Olives on South King Street, Slingsby's and Hero's on Ridgefield and Wood Street, but they were not to last long. As well as the Gay Centre on Bloom Street, by 1984 bars and clubs were mainly sited around what is now known as the Gay Village area. As well as the Rembrandt and the Union Pubs, the Thompson's Arms (now Central Park) next to Chorlton Street bus station, had gradually become a gay venue when the Campaign for Homosexual Equality (CHE) had rented the upstairs room in the late 70's. Also gay drag artist Glenn Stevens had taken over the licence for the Duke of Yorks Pub on Canal Street, which was soon renamed New York, then later "New York,New York". By 1985 the Bloom Street

Cafe had opened, there was the Archway on Whitworth Street West, High Society at 48 Princess Street and of course Napoleon's had survived the various attempts to close it.

From the late 60's there had also been a club on Oldham Street. Separate from the rest of the community, Dickens had a reputation like that of the Union Pub. Both catered for the gay person who was less well off. The Union was considered to be a 'spit and sawdust' style of bar, and accordingly:

> You only went up to Dickens or the Union if you were looking for a seedy place, somewhere a bit dodgy, but at least people talked to you there. (interview)

Both were very popular with working class women (mainly because they were amongst the very few venues which gave them entrance), and transvestites and transsexuals. The Union had a regular drag act from the early 70's, with an elderly 'queen' nicknamed "mother" miming to Shirley Bassey records. Both were places where rent boys were allowed in, and the clientele often dressed the part. Women would wear their bus driver and ambulance personnel jackets, men were welcome whatever their style or age. They had a reputation as places where those new to the scene would be made welcome and where they might well make a pick up.

Ironically just as the bars and clubs, in the late 60's, had originally grown around the area where cruising and cottaging would draw in customers, in the early 1980's as the rent scene had moved to the Sackville Street and Bloom Street area, which were originally considered very disreputable haunts, so the clubs and bars followed.

Building a Village

Since 1984, initiatives taken by Manchester City Council, combined with the setting up of a Gay Business Association, and the increasing politicisation of the gay community in the city - through AIDS awareness and the battle against Clause 28 have led to a substantial growth in the number of trades and venues catering for lesbians and gay men in what has become known as the Gay Village.

The city council, through the work of the Gay Men's Sub Committee have been encouraged to provide funding for the renovation of the canal side along Canal Street, to improve street lighting in the area and to make a pedestrianised area alongside the Union Pub. Planning permission and licences have been given for new bars and clubs. These have included La Cage on Bloom Street, The State, Follies, Rockies and Cafe Euro on

Whitworth Street, Austins and the Q Bar on Richmond Street, and Manto's on Canal Street.

Manchester's Gay Village is a result of the work and campaigns of all various interested parties: the city council, the club and bar owners and licensees, queer activists and queer consumers.

But most importantly in getting these groups to see their interests as common interests, let us not forget the role of the police. Just as in New York, in Manchester, one more raid was just one raid too often. When the police raided Napoleon's on the 17th November 1984, it is certain that they did not think that they would provide the key to revitalising the gay liberation movement in the city.

However despite this, when looking at what Gay clubs and bars there were in the 1970's there really are not many more in the 1990's despite the opening in 1992 of Cruz 101 - which has the biggest floor area of any gay club in Europe.

But now the atmosphere on the streets is very different - in the past gay people walked from the Union to Napoleons in fear and in isolation - in fact generally they didn't walk on the streets at all, because it was unsafe. Now in the 1/4 sq.mile of Manchester's gay village, everybody walks the street. One of the great attractions of the Village is that it is easy to move around, instead of being confined to one location for an evening, customers can walk easily from site to site. The fact of there being so many queer people using the area, means that individuals feel safer on the streets as they move around. So some things are better, but are some things worse?

Sex and Culture

Gayle Rubin (1984) said

> This culture always treats sex with suspicion. It construes and judges any sexual practice in terms of its worst possible expression. Sex is presumed guilty until proven innocent. (Rubin, 1984)

I want to reverse this and say "Queer sex treats culture with suspicion. It construes any cultural practice in terms of its worst possible expression. Culture is presumed guilty until proven innocent". The Gay Village 'idea' has promoted a marketplace in which queer people are now seen as cultural consumers, just another tribe amidst and like all other cultural consumers. In the past a Gay bar, was a safe place inside for lesbian, gay and other queer people - a place where you could finally be yourself - you could drop the mask. But now, the village is open to all. Everywhere you go there are straight people using the gay scene for entertainment (Manto's bar typifies this) - which means that for many gay people it is no longer a safe place inside to go, nor can you just be your (political) self. There has been a recent increase in 'mixed clubs' in the city where

> Different cultures and communities are brought together under the umbrella of drugs and dance music and subsequently people are forced to gain (or fain) increased awareness and respect for each other - gay culture is presented as more acceptable and respectable in a mixed club to those who would otherwise have been shocked at it. (Redway, 1992)

Politics no longer have a place in Manchester's Gay Village, it has become a balloon culture of celebration, as represented in the mixed clubs. Sometime, I must ask what we are celebrating - the deaths of so many of our friends?

Concurrently the American influence of the 'beautiful people' syndrome has invaded the Gay clubs. It has been around straight clubs for several years - but for young straight people that was OK, because the choice of clubs available meant that if you were not cool and trendy and hip, you could go to somewhere that was un-cool, un-trendy and un-hip - even the church youth club, could provide a place to meet others like yourself.

However for lesbians and gay men there are not the same number of choices, and if the scene is located in one such small geographical area, then it is likely that there are never going to be any more choices. Go out into Manchester's Gay Village now and gone are the bus conductresses uniforms, and the chiffon scarves of the queens - instead it is the time and age of the beautiful young people. But ironically beautiful young people don't need safe and tolerant places - because sex is always going to be easy for them; they are, after all, beautiful and desired.

But if you are not young and beautiful, how are you going to meet people to have sex with - which we should not deny has been for many the prime purpose of all night time cultures, straight or gay.

If you become alienated in the place you should be welcome before we know it there is going to be a need for a new Gay Liberation movement. Able bodied, white, beautiful young men have always had power and freedom, as such they all too easily fall into the trap of the offerings made by 'The freedom of the market place'. These people are now being offered extra venues (referred to here as the infiltrators), in which to spend their purchasing power . There has been realised an acceptable face to homosexuality - the young and the beautiful, who can be portrayed as being asexual, yet desirable.

In that way "FLESH" at the Hacienda was created, which is a great way of being liberal - at the same time as pushing up the takings on an otherwise slack Wednesday night. It's expensive enough to deter the old and ugly working class, but the 'nice gay boys' who buy apartments in the city centre and the warehouse projects will come and practice ideas of clean safe yet entertainingly camp sex, without ever actually doing it. The

> Mixed club .... instead of becoming positively interactive is just passively oppressive - no overt display of affection and you are alright. (Redway, 1992)

The 'nice gay boys' pay for the privilege of becoming the floor show for the straight audience. An audience which apparently desires them and what they represent, but which is hardly likely to agree to go to bed with them. Very safe sex !

But it is not really safe: firstly, gay people are being seen - straight people just are; secondly, those who go to FLESH who are straight walk out into a safe world, those who are lesbian or gay walk out into a dangerous world of queer bashers and sadistic policemen; thirdly: there are those gay men who do leave and go have 'unsafe' sex which may kill them.

'How safe is fashion?' because that is what the infiltrators are creating and then following. What happens when the straight world and its infiltrators lose interest, when the market has been saturated, when it is no longer new, original and attractive to bring lesbians and gay men into the safe straight world? When everybody can claim to be queer, because all sex is queer, even sleeping with someone of the opposite sex. At such a time, will the Gay Village have been eroded by the post capitalist straight world's desperate need to grab any market going, and when the boom is over will there be any safe place left for gay people?

Safe space was the original purpose of the gay scene, the club owners were gay, the users were gay - and they all slept together in the same bed - away from risk, and fear, they were safe, in a safe place, with safe people.

Interestingly it was only upon writing this, that I realised that at no time in the discussions around the work that the Manchester Institute for Popular Culture was doing on night time Manchester was it ever suggested that this discourse was ever more than a part of the discourse of night time Manchester. Yet where exactly is Manchester's night time economy situated? It may well be thriving down at the club, but for whose benefit, often tourists and those from out of town? Perhaps a gay discourse is more than a part of the discourse of night time Manchester, it is the centre of it and it encompasses all of the issues. 'Your' (straight) discourse is just part of 'our' (lesbian and gay) discourse.

A neo-marxist may interpret the culture of the infiltrating clubs in terms of the development of a higher stage of capitalism, marked by a greater degree of capital penetration and homogenization. At the same time it also produces a contradiction of increased cultural fragmentation. There occurs changes in the experience of space and time, and new modes of experience, subjectivity, and culture in Gramsci's ethical and cultural state.

Postmodernism's micropolitics and microtheories about the experience of gay people cannot explain how the development of a more liberal environment, with more open space and more accessibility can in the end, have produced less safe space and less accessibility. It is only through the macrotheories of the state and the consumer that the pressure on the individual to consent to his own coercion can be understood.

There has been reached a point where for the ease of processing the cultural consumer, a certain sameness develops everywhere - and we fall into the trap set by capital for us, we pretend we are the same, we become interchangeable for each other in the cultural process. We all are queer.

But the Gay scene is different, and some of us are comfortable with that difference. Such difference is attractive, in a time of sameness we all want difference. But straight culture cannot become 'queer' by adopting those aspects of a lesbian or gay lifestyle which are seen as being different or attractive. Once adopted those aspects become the same, part of the straight world, and that destroys the very essence of those differences. Differences that have a history of providing safe places.

Bibliography

Cox, A., Scott, D. (1984) *Gotcha, a case study of covert police surveillance*, Youth Development Trust, Manchester.

Dubermann, M.B., Vicinius, M., Chauncey, G., (1991) *Hidden from History, reclaiming the Gay and Lesbian past*, Penguin, London.

Duggan, L. (1992) "Making it perfectly queer", *Socialist Review*, Vol 22, No 1, Jan - Mar pp 11-32.

Forgacs, D. (1988) *A Gramsci Reader*, Lawrence and Wisehart, London.

Galloway, B. (ed) (1983) *Prejudice and Pride*, Routledge and Kegan Paul, London.

Gough, J., Macnair, M. (1985) *Gay Liberation in the Eighties*, Pluto Press, London.

Greenlees, A. (1991) "The Andrew R Greenlees Column", *Scene Out*, Feb, No 23, p 16.

Hatch, P. (1991) "The regulation of Male homosexuality", *Strangeways Newsletter*, Summer, Centre for Studies in Crime and Social Justice, Edgehill.

Jeffreys, S. (1990) *Anticlimax*, The Womens'Press, London.

Lowry, A. (1985) "Good For Business Bad for gay Lib?", *Mancunian gay*, March, No 40, pp 10-11.

O'Donovan, K. (1985) *Sexual Divisions in Law*, Weidenfeldt and Nicholson, London.

Redway, P. (1993) "Talking about a Liberation", *Pulp*, October, Iss 2, MMSU, Manchester.

Part II: Tales of the cities

The city is an organic creature, it changes, grows, parts of it die and are then renewed. But none of that happens without its inhabitants; without the human face the city reverts to the countryside, nature takes it back. In that way the city is parasitic, it thrives and survives on us who as Lilliputian figures in our Gotham City landscapes hurry and scurry to its bidding.

But the size of the city is such that we, who are the human face of the city, can rarely associate as a single community. The immensity of such an organisational task would require all our energies, and it is unlikely that we would have the time and energy left over to maintain the very fabric of the space we have constructed. So we organise and we associate into smaller communities within the larger. The city has many such communities of which the gay community is but one. Each community takes over the creation, maintenance and support of its own area and its own interests. These communities will, as a result, often find themselves at odds with each other as their interests, and the space in which they happen, clash or coincide. A city is not a result of some great overview; planned towns are just that - towns, cities are much more. They are a conglomeration of interests, desires and actions.

The next three chapters look at how the interests, desires and actions of the gay communities in three cities have adopted and changed space, and given it a sense of place.

3 Community with/out pro-pink-uity

Hans Almgren

It is a well-known fact that lesbians and gays for a long time have concentrated in certain areas. But while social sciences have well-developed theories about the outcome of social structures on urban space, lesbian and gay lives have mostly been ignored. To the extent that social scientists have acknowledged the socio-spatial aspects of lesbians and gay men, they have largely documented the visibility of gay spaces and culture that emerged with the "explosion of things gay" (Marotta, 1981) in the 1970s. In these studies, the particularities facing women, blacks and other ethnic minorities and the poor were often ignored.

But to conceptualize whole neighbourhoods as lesbian and gay, is to forget that the neighbourhood is also used by heterosexuals, who have always been the majority of users and residents. There are, however, particular spaces, streets, buildings or blocks that may temporarily transcend hegemonic heterosexuality. The asymmetrical power between heterosexual and gay access to public space was probably best summarized by Carl Wittman (1972) when he wrote that "we have formed a ghetto, out of self protection. And it is a ghetto, because it is still theirs."

Studies of lesbians, in contrast to gay men, have tended to focus on social networks, rather than on spaces created or appropriated. This tendency is likely an outcome of the history of lesbian - and women's in general - organisation, since public women-only spaces always have been few. Manuel Castells' (1983, p 140) dismissal of women as inherently 'placeless' therefore shoots beside the target. The absence of visible lesbian spaces cannot be an indicator that such socio-spatial organising does not exist, because lesbian spaces do exist and are visible to whomever they are visible to.

The dismissal of lesbians serves here to illustrate the slippery inclusion and the exclusion of those who have often been marginalised as 'others' within a marginalised category. Otherness has not only led lesbians and gays to be ignored in science - from the outside - but many lesbians and gays have also been marginalised within what often is referred to as 'the lesbian and gay community.' Gay men have often ignored omnipresent gender structures. White gay people have often ignored the particularities facing gay people of colour. The wealthy have often ignored the poor. But it is not the differences that separate, Audre Lorde (1990, p 282) once argued, rather it is our refusal to recognize them.

Although recognition of differences is of particular focus in current 'queer' theoretical thought, and we now are theoretically better equipped to understand how a multitude of social axes forms socio-spatial communities, there is a lack of empirical investigation of the complex relations between sexuality and space. Through a knowledge of how community members experience the community, how its margins and core relate to each other, and how it reflects and overlaps with other communities, it is possible to bridge a theoretical and empirical gap in the understanding of lesbian and gay shared and disjunct experiences. Thereby it would be possible to sharpen theories about 'communities' that includes dynamics of diversity and unity.

The purpose of this paper is to develop a critique of one concept that is frequently used to denote people for whom a same-sex desire is of an active every-day importance. The critique targets the static conceptualization of 'the lesbians and gay community,' and argues for a rethinking of 'community,' so that it may be useful in praxis.

Method

There is no reliable method to measure how lesbian and/or gay a neighbourhood is, nor is it possible to find a representative sample of lesbians and gay men. Since a conceptual problem arise with sexual categories, an analogy put forward by Richard Goldstein (1993) between the lesbian and gay community and religious congregations is quite effective in understanding communities. Goldstein writes that:

> ... people become gay when they choose to view their homosexuality as good. ...On the other hand, lesbians and gay men who don't think gay is good live very differently. ...When pressed, many of these lesbians and gay men insist they aren't gay. We tend to see their protestations as symptoms of denial, but maybe they are genuine assertions of a negative attitude toward homosexuality - what might be called a failure of faith. ...There are many lesbians and gay men - bisexuals who aren't gay, because they stand outside the faith. What's more, other bi's do have the faith, and they are demanding a place within the community. ...A condition has become a community; a movement is becoming a faith.

46

A label based on a faith is clearly different from a label based on a desire, regardless of whether it is acted upon or not. The faith is becoming less and less defined by sex, and more and more by an attitude towards sexuality, about - again I quote Goldstein (ibid) - "a congeries of belief that organises gayness as a way of being".

Although it may be possible to find a representative sample of self-identified lesbians and gays, neither will such a sample be reliable. Many gay people are out in some environments, but not to everyone and everywhere. "Many lesbians separate different activity spheres and hence identities in space" (Valentine, 1993, p 243), which is likely to be true for many gay men as well. A community of lesbians and gays can thus only be formed in an environment in which self-identified lesbians and gays are out to each other and congregate. By being out to each other, lesbians and gays not only construct community, but also lesbian and gay space.

In the United States, neither religious affiliation, nor lesbians and gays are accounted for in any official source of data. I have argued elsewhere (Rothenberg and Almgren, 1992), that one does not have to count everyone to get a sense of lesbian and gay space. Rather, lesbian and gay spaces, places and neighbourhoods can be perceived and anecdotally substantiated. If gayness is accepted as a faith, or a way of being, then we can also accept that it is not possible to find a representative sample of lesbians and gay men. Nor is it for my purpose desirable. What instead can be achieved, is finding a sample that can account for the communal dynamics of believers. One method with the potential to do so, is the case study method.

Robert Yin (1989, p 21) points out that although case studies can not be used in the search for generalisations of

> ... populations or universes, [they] are generalisable to theoretical propositions.

He further argues that the

> unique strength of the case study method is its ability to deal with a full variety of evidence, [that] .... even certain journalistic efforts can qualify. (ibid, p 20-24)

Through case studies in progress of lesbian and gay communal forms in New York, I have conducted interviews. Below I will quote from some of the interviews to illustrate some of the problems of the community concept, and that individuals, unlike community investigators, have no particular problem in sensing where and what their communities consist of. The interviews should not be regarded as final results, nor as representative for any social, cultural or spatially localized group.

With more than 7 million people, large groups of ethnic, racial, lesbian an gay minorities, New York has the critical mass and mix that supports different forms of lesbian and gay 'communities.' The neighbourhood primarily in discussion here, is that of Jackson Heights, Queens. With almost two million people, the borough of Queens is large enough to support a lesbian and gay community of its own, away from the better known lesbian and gay centres in Manhattan.

But in order to understand the questions raised, we have to understand why 'community' is so problematic when used for and among lesbians and gay men. To that I now will turn.

The Problem of Community

> Anyone who knows the gay community is aware that it stands
> for many things, some quite contradictory.
> > - Richard Goldstein (1993)

Definitions of communities tend to be as broad as is the usage of the concept. Traditionally a community was defined as an area where the social life of an individual was indistinguishable from her or his place of residence. With increasing urbanization and mobility, people became less tied to their residential neighbourhoods, and could instead associate at convenient meeting places, with whomever they share a "communality" (McClenahan, 1946). Although these 'communities without propinquity' are not necessarily based in the neighbourhoods people live, Loyd and Rowntree (1978, p 79) writes, they are

> not nonspatial communities, ...for they do have places or nodes
> in which community members may meet.

Lesbians and gays have in some cases created highly visible and recognisable spaces and localised communities. In these cases, communality has recreated the spatial communities urbanization once supposedly dissolved. Epstein (1987, p 39) argues that the gay and lesbian community has in many respects come to resemble ethnic communities:

> To the extent that the gay community has succeeded in creating
> new institutional supports that link individuals into the
> community and provide their lives with a sense of meaning,
> gays may now be more 'ethnic' than the original groups.

48

Unlike ethnic communities, however, lesbians and gays are, in general, neither born into gay neighbourhoods, nor into gay social groups. While there is a lesbian and gay history (see e.g. Katz, 1976, and Duberman et al., 1989) there is no 'homeland' to long for, no collective language or memory. Instead, these have to be produced and reproduced, discovered and cognitively mapped in each generation and culture.

Implicity the community concept reduces complex identities to the least common denominator and amplifies the differences between the members of a community and whatever there is outside. The effect is that communities tend, by their static conceptualization, to be defined at their centres and viewed in isolation, while I suggest that they instead are in flux, amorphous, interconnected, and overlapping. Consider Ulf Hannertz' (1992, p.73) critique of the subcultural concept, a critique equally applicable to the community concept. He writes that the definition of subcultures tends to be internalist, that

> the isolation of subcultures can only be a matter of degree. ...Much writing on subcultures looks mostly inward, toward their distinctive cores rather than toward their interfaces with whatever is outside, which ...exaggerates isolation. ...As 'pieces,' [subcultures] are all of one kind, all largely homogeneous in their internal characteristics, and all hard-edged. ...Subcultures can overlap in individuals, who may not keep them entirely compartmentalized within their perspectives, with varied consequences for overall cultural organisation. ...The idea of subcultural hard edges [does not] seem particularly helpful.

This critique raises the question to what extent a community - based on a shared faith can be isolated from other social structures like class, gender, race, ethnic origin, age, culture, and religion - just to mention a few - and be subsumed under the umbrella term of 'the lesbian and gay community.' Chela Sandoval (1984, p 726) writes:

> There is no single sex-role socialization that holds constant for all women; class, culture, race and sex intersects in various ways to produce different kinds of women, lesbians and lesbian communities.

Thus the community discourse, like the subcultural, falsely implies unity and homogeneity. The effect is that differences and diversity within the given community become marginalised. The problem arises in particular with the scale to which the community concept is applied. Scale of communities are poorly conceptualised. 'The lesbian and gay community' tends to refer to universes, be it global, national, or city-wide. But the larger the spatial scale a community is assumed at, the fewer shared communalities can be expected.

In order to overcome the scale problem of any community, one can study how people who identify themselves as lesbian or gay create communities. An alternative to embarking on studies of a priori defined lesbian and gay communities, is to ask how lesbians and gays organise socially and spatially. Such questions may reveal to what extent there are local communities, if these communities are cores of their own or marginalised in relation to cores elsewhere, or if multiple identities perhaps establish several communities that not merely are juxtaposed, but overlapping, in one and the same space. Through the example of Jackson Heights, a neighbourhood in which lesbians and gays have created communal forms, I will generate some questions that may be further explored.

Lesbian and Gay Neighbourhoods in New York

Of all New York's neighbourhoods, Greenwich Village is the one most obviously and publicly identified with lesbians and gay men. The Village is home to the Lesbian and Gay Community Services Center as well as several other institutions. It is taken for granted as being the home of New York's lesbian and gay community, but perhaps more so for heterosexuals, than by lesbians and gay themselves. Anyone who has visited the neighbourhood on a Saturday night when it serves as one of New York's entertainment centres, knows that the 'gayness' is at best confined to a few (semi) public spaces. Yet the neighbourhood is represented in the City Council by an out gay man, and in the State Assembly by an out gay woman. If that is a measure of power, then it can be argued that gay voices have officially entered the centre.

In a discussion of centre and margin of the lesbian and gay community, the community activities in a neighbourhood like Greenwich Village will thus rather represent the centre to which lesbians and gays come from all over the city, and indeed, from all over the world (Parish 1990). Yet it would be a mistake to assume that all gay people wish to live in a gay-identified neighbourhood. Evelyn Hooker (1967) found, in Los Angeles in the 1950s, not only that gay men clustered spatially, but that

> the population is also distributed widely throughout the city and its suburbs since other factors than association affect the choice of residence.

Historic research in New York has shown that diversity of gay scenes indicated a social and spatial distancing, in particular based on differences of gender and class, as early as the late 19th Century (Chauncey, 1989).

Less known as a lesbian and gay neighbourhood is Jackson Heights, Queens. In 1991 it splashed into the open and onto the pages of the local city newspapers. The catalyst was the murder of Julio Rivera, a Latin gay man. The New York Times, previously known to be squeamish in reporting about lesbian and gay issues (Signorile 1992), devoted lengthy coverage to the trial - and to the gay community of Jackson Heights. The Times reported that the area

> with little outside notice [has] become home to the city's second-largest gay community,

that the trial

> has given a strong public voice to gay New Yorkers outside the largely white world of the city's traditional gay centre, Greenwich Village,

and that it has been the home of a gay community for more than 25 years (Lord, 1991).

Martin Levine's (1979) mapping of 'Gay Ghettos' in major U.S. cities, revealed a clustering of gay institutions in Jackson Heights. Building in ghetto definitions of the Chicago School of sociologists, Levine argued that while New York's West (Greenwich) Village met the definitions, Jackson Heights did not. It lacked a dominant gay 'culture area,' and a concentration of gay peoples homes. Weinberg and Williams (1974), who had conducted research on gay neighbourhoods in New York in the late 1960s, do not mention Jackson Heights. Neither did any neighbourhoods outside Manhattan show up as particularly gay in the early 1960s, with the exception of Brooklyn Heights, a "gay suburbia popular with 'young marrieds'" (Helmer 1963).

Yet the absence of information of a neighbourhood as lesbian or gay, cannot be used a positive evidence that it is not. One informant is aware of gay presence in Jackson Heights since the 1950s, because he was as a child told to stay away from certain places where gay cruising took place (Interview 1). Presence of lesbians and gays can, on the other hand, be positively proved and their communal dynamics accounted for.

Lesbians, Gays and Community in Jackson Heights

> In fact, ...there is enough lavender tile in Jackson Heights to
> cover the whole U.S.
> - Mr. Lopardi about the commonly found Art Deco
> bathrooms, quoted by Roach (1983)

Jackson Heights is one of New York's most diverse neighbourhoods.
Popular media have called it

> the most polyglot, polyethnic urban quarter in the world
> (Sokolov, 1991)

The neighbourhood is the home to so many Colombians that it in Colombia
is called "the colony" (Roach, 1983), and "Little Colombia" in New York
(Dao, 1992).

Before the turn of the century, Jackson Heights did not exist, there were
only wide open farm land and fields. The first subway line opened in 1917,
and with it, Jackson Heights came within easy reach of Manhattan. The cooperative housing developments were among the first in the city, surrounded
by golf courses and tennis fields. By the late 1950s, little available land was
left (Karatzas 1990). Charlie Chaplin once lived in the neighbourhood
(Orlean 1993).

In the 1960s U.S. immigration quotas were loosened, and immigrants from
primarily Latin America and Asia found a home in and around Jackson
Heights. Of the total population of one hundred thousand living in the
census tracts surrounding the area's gay bars and Roosevelt Boulevard - the
main strip - between the Brooklyn-Queens Express way and Junction
Boulevard, Latinos constitute 44 per cent (U.S. Bureau of the Census, 1990).
The largest single ethnic group is Colombian. Apart from the Latin
neighbourhood flavour, that of Asian Indians stand out. Along 74th Street,
Indians have established an enclave with 82 establishments and requested to
have the area officially designated as "Little India" (Myers 1993). Yet few
Indians live in the neighbourhood. In fact, they are only 2 per cent of the
population in the census tracts within which the commercial enclave is
established (U.S. Bureau of the Census, 1990).

Lesbian and gay organisations in Queens have a disrupted history. In the
late 1970s and early 1980s, several organisations developed and specialised
for different groups. These organisations co-operated in lobbying efforts to
get New Yorks City's gay rights bill to pass, but eventually they dissolved.
A new wave of activism surged after Julio Rivera's murder, and through
local attempts to create a 'gay-winnable' city council district in 1991
(Queens Pride Guide 1993, p.8; 18). The unwillingness of the police to

classify the murder as a bias crime, made "Julio Rivera's name ...[a] rallying cry in New York's gay community," and in response the borough saw its first Gay *Rights* march ever (Pooley 1991, p 38, *my emphasis*). Out of the political activism, QGLU, Queens Gays and Lesbians United, took form (Queens Pride Guide 1993, p 18). The organisation has since worked together with the local police precinct to sensitize neighbourhood officers (Hernandez 1993). A Queens School Board's refusal to accept the 'Rainbow Curriculum,' that among many things would have taught children that families come in different forms, increased activism. "Partially in response to the campaign of hate and lies by a bigoted ...community school board president," offspring of QGLU organised Queens' first Gay *Pride* march and block party in Jackson Heights, June 6, 1993 (Queens Pride Guide, 1993, p 5, *my emphasis*).

Although an organisation like QGLU is open to everybody, and has managed to attract both gay women and men, its efforts to reach out beyond the borough's Anglo gay population has not been equally successful:

> Latino gays are not well connected to the gay community, they do not often identify as a part of it. (Interviewee 1, Anglo Male, living in Jackson Heights).

Or as someone else expressed it:

> In Jackson Heights, there are 2 types of gay people: those who hang out at bars and those who has been around longer, these [latter] are largely Anglos (Interviewee 2, Anglo Male, living in Jackson Heights).

The neighbourhood's large Asian population is not well represented at the bars:

> There is no connection to the Asians in Jackson Heights. There are very few Asians that come to the bars. The bars are Anglo and Latino, and ...connections between Anglos and Latinos are very subtle. Latinos who to American parties are those who are integrated, those who have adjusted to American culture. (colombian Male living in Jackson Heights).

If gay Latinos and Anglos hardly mix socially, nor share most of the bars, it suggests that the gay communality is weaker than language and cultural differences. If so, then there are arguably two gay communities sharing the same neighbourhood.

To the extent there is a Latin - or Colombian as it often is suggested - gay community, it is largely centred in and around the bars. Within a few blocks, at least 8 gay bars are located, several of which are exclusively Latin. In these the music played is Latin, the jukeboxes are stocked with Latin records, the dances danced are merengue and salsa. But is a bar scene enough for creating a community? Some think it is, others do not:

> I have no sense of a Colombian gay community. Many people know each other's faces in the bars. If you know people at the bars, it is because you knew them from before, from the outside. Once can meet friends there, but not make friends. (Interviewee 4, Colombian Male, living in neighbouring Sunnyside).

The ambivalence about community is also expressed as not necessarily being tied to a spatial or social Colombian community:

> I'm Colombian, but I don't belong to the Colombian community. I sort of belong to the gay community in Manhattan. ..[In Jackson Heights] there is one [gay bar] that I go to ...when I really want to think of my past in Colombia. They play Colombian folk music. And I love it. [The neighbourhood] makes a difference for me. (Interviewee 5, Colombian Male living in Astoria, Queens).

> I think that the one most important [aspects of identity] in New York for me is to be gay, which is the reason I eventually moved to New York. I wanted to live in a place where I could be myself, where there was a community for gay men around me...And then being Colombian is very important. I may never go back there again to live, but it is the soul. (Interviewee 6, Colombian Male living in Manhattan).

Access to bars are, however, only a one-sided community function. Latinos also have other communal support functions that are shared between gay and straight regardless of their beliefs. Some of these communal functions have emerged in response to the AIDS epidemic.

AIDS has not left any neighbourhood in New York untouched. The particularities of a health crisis that faces minority populations have led to a development of programs to meet special needs. Gay Men's Health Crisis, GMHC, has outreach programs targeting Latinos. "Culture, educational levels and language create barriers, that scare people off if they are not approached in the right way", says Guillermo Vasquez, coordinator of Community Outreach and Education. He exemplifies with the brochures and workshops developed by GMHC, largely by and for a white middle-class male population. These cannot just be translated for a population that cannot identify with the message. If a brochure says 'See your doctor...,' it is not very helpful since they may not have one.

Luis Nieves-Rosa, HIV Counsellor of the Entre Hombres Project, Hispanic AIDS Forum, points to similar problems. The Hispanic AIDS Forum was started in 1985 by concerned Latinos of the effects of AIDS in the Latin community. Although Latinos have been affected since the beginning of the epidemic, few paid much attention to minorities at that time. It became important, says Mr. Nieves, to develop educational material in Spanish that was culturally targeting the Latin community.

In 1991 funds had become available to open an office of the Hispanic AIDS Forum in Jackson Heights. The location was determined by the incidence of Latino AIDS cases locally. Although the agency serves anyone, its target population is Latinos. Entre Hombres makes case assessments regarding insurance, immigration status, entitlements and medical care. In a referral program, other agencies and organisations that can provide the needed services are contacted. Not gay-identified Latinos acting upon homosexual desire are reached by cruising areas where anonymous sex takes place. When someone has gained their trust, Entre Hombres can hold safe-sex workshops for the person and his friends in the neutral and safe environment of a private home. The organisations do not single out illegal immigrants. Part of Entre Hombres' project, is to help them work on their legal status. Insurance funding is provided so that illegal aliens are not left out of medical care.

Services like those provided by GMHC and The Hispanic AIDS Project, are functions in which both the Latin community and the lesbian and gay community have investments. The services available to non-believers are made possible through the material location, and the programs also give non-believers access to the local community.

The Invisibility of Community

Other lesbians and gays in New York may not even have heard about the neighbourhood, or that it has a large gay population. One lesbian who grew up in neighbouring Sunnyside and whose mother lived in Jackson Heights, spontaneously mentioned Jackson Heights as one of the least gay neighbourhoods in the city. When she was told about New York Times' claim that the neighbourhood is home to New York's second largest gay community, her response was:

Get out of town! Honest, I've been hanging around that neighbourhood since I was 12 years old and never in my life have I thought of any gay community in Jackson Heights. I don't think there is a gay community from Queens that would congregate anywhere...I never thought of Queens as having any kind of gay community at all. (Interviewee 7, Anglo Lesbian in search of a residence in Manhattan).

As an anglo woman, and the relative absence of women in the anglo bars, her gender may have led her to not recognize the gayness of the neighbourhood since its semi public, and in particular anglo expressions, are male dominated. But perhaps more telling is her comment on knowing where and how to find communities:

I suppose you find what you're looking for in any place, but my experiences in Jackson Heights, ...that's not what we were there for. ...It may very well be a large community, they just don't advertise it much. (Interviewee 7, Anglo Lesbian).

One is likely to find what one is looking for in any neighbourhood, although it may be harder in some neighbourhoods than others. In the many sources of where to find lesbian and gay bars in New York, bars in minority neighbourhoods are blatantly absent. The listed bars where mostly African-Americans or Asians meet, are located in areas where few of these minorities live. There are, however, suggestions of lesbian and gay neighbourhoods and institutions, like bars, in neighbourhoods where mostly African-Americans live, but also that these are purposely hidden from the community at large. One explanation as to why they are kept secret is that Black people want to keep these bars Black. If they are listed in the lesbian and gay press, too many white men show up (Interviewee 8, African-American Male).

While lesbians and gay men may by oppressed because of being gay, it is no guarantee that those who are privileged in a racist, sexist, capitalist culture do not marginalize lesbians and gays who are not. One of the most contested and strongly criticised forms of gay oppression of other lesbians and gays is objectification.

The post-Stonewall white gay community of the 1980s was not seriously concerned with the existence of black and gay men except as sexual objects. In media and art the black male was given little representation except as a big, black dick (Hemphill, p xviii).

Colombian-American author Jaime Manrique made a similar point when I interviewed him:

> The reason gay people bond is because of sex. It is like the hatred between blacks and whites, white men are like slave owners. They didn't marry black women but having sex with them was fine. There is a lot of objectification going on in gay culture, and all cultures: Blondes who like Blacks or Latinos. It is just objectification going on in gay culture, and all cultures: Blondes who like Blacks or Latinos. It is just objectification of the other for sexual gratification. Actually, it is more prejudice, I think, with objectification, because the other person is not a person, but a type, an archetype.

In mapping lesbian and gay communities, there is a conflict between revealing information of importance for the arguments and information that interviewees prefer to keep hidden. As already argued, one does not have to count everybody, or thereby all communities or neighbourhoods to get a sense of lesbian and gay communal dynamics. Therefore sources about lesbian and gay communities can, at best, be suggestive (Almgren and Rothenberg 1992). The success of any study of lesbian and gay communities is dependent on the questions asked, rather than the availability of representative data. The question of why lesbian and gay minorities have reasons to hide particular institutions, spaces and places from the community at large will provide more insight into the communal dynamics - or lack thereof - than the particular location themselves.

Even if there are few connections between gay Latinos and gay Anglos, it cannot be argued that they are not part of New York's lesbian and gay community, the neighbourhood, or share communalities with other Latinos or Anglos. Communities are not discrete entities where participation in one automatically disqualifies one from participating in the other. Social and spatial distancing between Anglos and Latinos, similar to that in Jackson Heights, have been suggested elsewhere (Carrier 1992, Lockard 1986). The quotes used here illustrate, if nothing else, the elusiveness of the concept of community.

A distinction can be made between a group appropriating a space within the lesbian and gay communality, and a gay group appropriating a space within a neighbourhood. One can thus ask if a group of gay Latinos has established a core of their own in a Latin neighbourhood, if the group is marginalised within the lesbian and gay community of New York, neither or both. Perhaps the best answer for now is that 'community' is at best a relative concept.

Keeping the Baby

Against the theoretical background about cores and margins within the lesbian and gay community, it is hardly surprising that lesbian and gay localities are diverse. But what also is evident, is that people who have the faith, do find support in their local communal forms.

My suggestion is that studies of different lesbian and gay communities, in which not only the shared belief but also other social axes like genes, class, race and ethnic origin are underlying the communal dynamics, by themselves address the problem of the scale. There is a community of some sort entered in the neighbourhood of Jackson Heights ,and the individuals who are the community knows best at what scale it functions. If sexuality is not isolated from other social structures, it can be argued that there is more than one community in the neighbourhood, each of which is sharing more communalities than a faith. When communities are defined a priori, we not only have problems in locating them, we also erect new boundaries and new hard edges, although at new scales. The solution may lie in not defining communities a priori but let people suggest them to us. Community is therefore a useful concept when applied to the social space people construct for themselves in physical space, and the social organisation that is made possible by that social space constructed.

Throwing out the Bath Water

Hard edged, bounded committees are problematic, because, as Trinh T. Minh-ha (1990, p 331) has argued,:

> there cannot be any grand totalising integration without massive suppression, which is a way of recirculating the effects of domination.

Any community based on a centred definition excluding differences and margins will therefore fail in becoming a successful mass movement.

A starting point for recognising differences, is to throw out the homogeneous notion of the community discourse, and reconceptulize 'community' so that racism, sexism and ethnocentrism can be addressed. It is evident that we need to throw out the communal rhetoric, when its application marginalizes.

We need a conceptualization of community that, in Gayatri Spivak's (1990, p 381) wording,:

point(s) at the irreducibility of the margin in all explanations. That ...not merely reverse but displace the distinction between margin and centre.

We need to rethink communities in a way that does away with the normative hegemony, but keeps the possibility to affiliate and recognize our differences. We need to be reminded that there are centres in the margin, and margins in the centre. We need a concept that denotes a fractured, fragile and fragmented unity. We need a concept that throws the bath water out, but keeps the baby.

The Miami Theory Collective (1991) has rethought what the discourse of community does to differences. They call for a new concept that "is not a referenial sign but a call to appeal" (Singer 1991). These communities do not have defined boundaries or hard edges, but are at 'loose ends'. But a concept alone does not do much. We also need empirical data to build knowledge on how the core and margin relates to each other, what core to what margin, on what scale, how, where and why. These questions can be addressed by exploring lesbian and gay communities in the Jackson Heights all over the world. Such a grounded empirical approach both has the potential to bridge a gap to theory, and serve as a critique of homogeneity. With the help of all the Jackson Heights everywhere, we can throw the bath water out over all that lavender tile.

Bibliography

Interviews and information: Author Jaime Manrique. Luis Nieves, Entre Hombres Project of the Hispanic AIDS Forum. Guillermo Vasquez, GMHC.

Almgren, H. and Rothenberg, T. (1992) *This Must Be the Place: Seeking the Spatial Lesbian/Gay Community*. Paper presented at the annual meeting of the Association of American Geographers, San Diego, California.

Carrier, J. (1992) "Miguel: Sexual Life History of a Gay Mexican American", In Herdt, G. (ed.) *Gay Culture in America: Essays from the Field*. Beacon Press, Boston.

Chauncey, G. (1989) *Gay New York: Urban Culture and the making of a male world, 1890-1940*. PhD Dissertation, Yale University.

Dao, J. (1992) *Land of Magic in Heart of Queens. Others See Grit; Colombians Find Bogota on Roosevelt Ave, New York Times*, October 9.

Duberman, M.B., Vicinus, M. and Chauncey, G. Jr. (eds.) (1989) *Hidden from History, Reclaiming the Gay and Lesbian Past*. NAL Books, New York

Epstein, S. (1987) "Gay Politics, Ethnic Identity: The Limits of Social Constructionism", *Socialist Review*, Vol 17, No 93/94.

Goldstein, R. (1993) "Faith, Hope and Sodomy. Gay Liberation Embarks on a Vision quest", *Village Voice*, 29 June 1993, pp 21-23; 19-30.

Hannertz, U. (1992) *Cultural Complexity, Studies in the Social Organisation of Meaning*, Columbia University Press, New York.

Helmer, W. (1963) "New York's 'middle-class' Lesbians and gay men", *Harper's Magazine*, March, Vol 226, No 1354.

Hemphill, E. (1991) Introduction, in Hemphill, E. and Beam, J. (ed., resp convinced by) *Brother to Brother. New Writings by Black Gay Men*, Alyson Publications, Boston.

Hernandez, R. (1992) "Healing Wounds and Seeking Understanding, Police and Gay Residents of the 115th Precinct Work Together to Find Common Ground", *New York Times*, 19 April.

Hooker, E. (1967) The Homosexual Community. In: Gagnon, J. and Simon, W. (eds) *Sexual Deviance*, Harper and Row, New York.

Karatzas, D. (1990) *Jackson Heights. A Garden in the City. The History of America's First Garden and Cooperative Apartment Community*, privately published.

Katz, Jonathan N. (1976) *Gay American History: Lesbians and Gay Men in the U.S.A*, Thomas Y. Cromwell, New York.

Levine M. (1979) Gay Ghetto, *Journal of Homosexuality*, Vol 4(4), Summer.

Lockard, D. (1986) "The Lesbian Community : An Anthropological Approach", *Journal of Homosexuality*, 11 (3-4), pp. 83-95.

Lorch, D. (1991) "An Unlikely Martyr Focuses Gay Anger. Jackson Heights Slaying Galvanizes a Community That Had Prized Privacy", *New York Times* 11 Nov, B1.

Lorde, A. (1990) "Age, Race, Class and Sex: Women Redefining Difference", in: Ferguson, R.,Gever, M., Min-ha, T., and West, C. (eds). *Out There: Marginalisation and Contemporary Cultures*, MIT Press, Cambridge, MA.

Loyd, B. and Rowntree, L. (1978) "Radical Feminists and Gay Men in San Francisco : Social Space in Dispersed Communities", in Lanegran, D. and Palm, R. (eds) *An Invitation to Geography*, McGraw Hill, New York.

Marotta, T. (1981) *The Politics of Homosexuality. How lesbians and gay men have made themselves a political and social force in modern America*, Houghton Mifflin Company, Boston.

McClenahan, B. (1946) "The Communality: The Urban Substitute for the Traditional Community" *Society and Social Research*, Vol 30, pp.264-274.

Miami Theory Collective (1991) (eds.) *Community at Loose Ends*, University of Minnesota Press, Minneapolis.

Minh-ha, T. (1990) "Cotton and Iron", in Ferguson, Gever, R.M., Min-ha, T., and West, C., (eds.) *Out There: Marginalization and Contemporary Cultures*, MIT Press, Cambridge, MA.

Myers, S. (1993) "Bazaar With The Feel of Bombay, Right in Queens", *New York Times*, 4 January, p B1;10.

Orlean, S. (1993) "All Mixed Up", *The New Yorker*. 22 June , pp 90-104.

Parish L. (1990) *Testimony before the New York City Districting Commission*, Public Hearing at Intermediate School 131. 1 November 1990. Unpublished document available from The Empire State Pride Agenda.

Pooley, E. (1991) "With Extreme Prejudice. A Murder in Queens Exposes Frightening Rise of Gay-Bashing", *New York*, 8 April.

Queens Pride Guide (1993)

Roach M. (1983) "If You're Thinking of Living in: Jackson Heights", *New York Times* 23 January.

Rothenberg, T. and Almgren, H. (1992) *Social Politics of Space and Place in New York City's Lesbian and Gay Communities*, Paper presented at the International Geographic Congress, Washington, DC, August 1992.

Sandoval, C. (1984) "Comment on Krieger's Lesbian Identity and Community : Recent Social Science Literature", *Signs: Journal of Women in Culture and Society*, (9)4.

Signorile, M. (1992) "Out at The New York Times", *The Advocate* (part 1) 602, 5 May; (part 2) 603, 19 May.

Singer, L. (1991) "Recalling a Community at Loose Ends", in Miami Theory Collective (eds.) *Community at Loose Ends*, University of Minnesota Press, Minneapolis.

Sokolov, R. (1991) "Small Worlds. The City's Ethnic Enclaves are amazing Cornucopias of Tastes of all Nations", *New York*, Vol 24, No 50 (23-30 December).

Spivak, G. (1990) "Explanation and Culture: Marginalia", in Ferguson, Gever, R.M., Min-ha, T., and West, C. (eds.) *Out There : Marginalization and Contemporary Cultures*, MIT Press, Cambridge, MA.

U.S. Bureau of Census (1990) *Census of Population and housing*, Summary Tape File 3A.

Valentine G. (1992) "Negotiating and Managing Multiple Sexual Identities: Lesbian Time-Space Strategies", *Transactions. Institute of British Geographers*, 18, pp 237-248.

Weinberg, M. and Williams, C. (1974) *Male homosexuals: Their Problems and Adaptions*, Oxford University Press, New York.

Wittman, C. (1972) "Refugees from Amerika: A Gay Manifesto", in McCaffrey, J (ed.) *The Homosexual Dialectic*, Prentice Hall, Englewood Cliffs, NJ.

Yin, R (1989) *Case Study Research. Design and Methods*, Sage Publications, Newbury Park, CA.

4 Gentrification by gay male communities: A case study of Toronto's Cabbagetown

Anne-Marie Bouthillette

As part of the growing expression of lifestyle in the urban environment, gay men are forming an urban presence which has an increasingly visible impact on the landscape. In particular, gays have played an important role in the so-called "urban renaissance" gentrification. Writers interested in the field of gentrification have often noted, if only as an aside, the impact of gay communities on gentrification, whether in creating a long-lasting, stable gay community, or merely sparking further renewal of a neighbourhood. However, very little has been written specifically with respect to gay gentrification.

Earlier work includes Castells (1983), who states that, in the case of San Francisco, a long established gay city, gays have "definitely improved the quality of housing through repairs, remodelling and excellent maintenance" (Castells:1983, 158). He recognizes that every incoming urban group has an impact on urban housing, and acknowledges that gays are different from any other such group in that, even as a marginalized community, they have managed to raise the value of their territory. Clay (1979) also notes that many observers he has interviewed and/or surveyed have mentioned the substantial presence of homosexuals in the early stages of gentrification. Pattison (1983) does the same, and suggests that gays sought out gentrifiable space almost unconsciously. Indeed, he proposes that they tend to seek social environments where they will not be conspicuous, and that run-down inner-city (ie. gentrifiable) neighbourhoods are inclined to possess this characteristic. Thus, he sees gay gentrification as a near-inadvertent outcome of social constraints working against them, and as an unconscious affirmation of their right to existence. Yeates (1990) observes that homosexual men tend to locate in low-income downtown locations (Yeates:1990, 167), and acknowledges that the vibrancy of gay communities has frequently led to the redevelopment of their quarters. He therefore, if only sketchily, links gay gentrification to lifestyle motivations.

Perhaps the only exception to this reticence to discuss more fully the role of homosexual men in the urban landscape is the article by Lauria and

65

Knopp (1985), "Towards an Analysis of the Role of Gay Communities in the Urban Renaissance", where the authors present several instances of gentrification by this community, and propose certain clues as to why this occurs. They finally conclude the article by challenging urban geographers to probe the reasons why they gentrify. This would, hopefully, generate a theory of gay gentrification, thus legitimizing the existence, and importance, of the geography of homosexuality. This paper will follow Lauria & Knopp's cue, and explore gentrification by the homosexual community, using the case of Toronto's Cabbagetown neighbourhood. At least one theory describing gay gentrification has been proposed (Bouthillette: 1992), based on the assumption that marginalized groups are relegated to, and sometimes select, marginalized spaces (see Winchester & White: 1988). It argues that gay men have the economic ability and the desire to upgrade these spaces and, in essence, gentrify. This implies that, unlike most other marginalized groups, homosexual men are in a position to reshape not only the landscape they inhabit, but also influence the social, political and economic systems which govern it. The City of Toronto has itself experienced gay gentrification, and has felt the influence of this particular population in the last decade (and continues to do so). As such, it forms an ideal focus for this essay.

Methodology

The literature used came from various sources of knowledge. Due to the relatively novel nature of gay geographies as an area of study, much of the task of researching it involves synthesizing sources in geography, sociology and cultural studies among others. This broad literary framework is thus reflected the observations and conclusions offered in this essay. In addition, the lack of explicit information on the topic at hand, namely Toronto's gay community, necessitated much empirical research.

This empirical portion of the research consisted mainly of detailed, taped and transcribed interviews with eight (8) gay men and one lesbian woman, as well as one City of Toronto planner. The central eight informants represented a variety of occupational backgrounds (all white-collar professional, however), and all resided in Cabbagetown or Riverdale - all were gentrifiers. They were all contacted using a "snowball" method - friends and friends of friends of a gay municipal politician. In addition, I relied on the testimony, research and support of a gay colleague and real estate agent, who also put me in touch with three additional gay real estate agents. All these testimonies were helpful in many ways, including in helping to formulate a chronology of the development of the gay ghetto and of the gentrification of Cabbagetown, as well as in determining the motivations behind the individual decision to gentrify.

Gay Toronto

As Canada's recognized leading urban centre for gay life, Toronto is home to the country's most elaborate gay community. Located in Toronto's South Midtown area, with its core at the intersection of Church and Wellesley streets, the "gay ghetto" holds a vast assortment of bars, restaurants, stores, services and housing (high-rise apartments, co-ops and condominiums), all geared towards the particular needs of this population. In fact, planning authorities have recently recognized this area as the "Church Street Area of Special Identity", a designation which entails the strengthening of the retail function of the area, the protection of residential usage, and guidelines and incentives for retail development and improved streetscapes.

However, relatively little gay gentrification has occurred in the ghetto proper: rather, an adjacent neighbourhood, Cabbagetown, has seen the bulk of this type of gentrification. Another neighbourhood, Riverdale, immediately east of Cabbagetown, has also experienced gay gentrification in the recent past, but of a very different nature and, as such, will not be included in the core of this study. Rather, a brief discussion will follow in an effort to contrast the different character of each neighbourhood.

The main reason for the ghetto not having gentrified as extensively as Cabbagetown is the absence of much "gentrifiable" housing stock: as already mentioned, the great majority of housing there takes the form of multi-unit structures. Although some single-family homes do exist in the neighbourhood, the stock was too limited, in the words of a real estate agent and fellow researcher,

> to create a revitalizing street-oriented neighbourhood. [The] housing stock [was] too erratic to create a 'neighbourhood feeling' like in Cabbagetown. [The] housing stock [was also] probably more expensive on these streets than in Cabbagetown when the gentry started renovating. (personal letter)

In addition, the gay ghetto was not widely identified as such - at least, not by outsiders - until the early eighties, well after the bulk of the gentrification of Cabbagetown had taken place.

The Gay Ghetto - A Brief History

The area known as Toronto's Gay Ghetto stretches roughly from Bay Street to the west, Bloor Street to the north, Sherbourne Street to the east and Gerrard Street to the south in the city's Midtown district (see Fig. 1). Among the residents, it is commonly known as "Church-Wellesley", named after the two streets which intersect at its core, and forms the hub of gay life in Toronto: with an abundance of bars, restaurants and specialty food stores, as well as facilities such as the YMCA and the "519" community centre, it is the gathering place for Toronto's homosexuals when they need/want to participate in their own cultural minority. Yet, clearly, this was not always the case.

As in most North American cities, the visible emergence of Toronto's gay population came about in the late 1960's, after the Stonewall Riots. However, in Toronto's case, gay men were, rather unconsciously, being drawn to the Church-Wellesley area much earlier than this (as early as the late 1950's). This was primarily because it was one of the first downtown areas to have large quantities of apartments (high- and low-rise), of which City Park Apartments was the first, well-suited to their household size (ie. single) and their urban lifestyle. This influx of apartment buildings came as a result of the opening of the Yonge Street subway line, along which population nodes (corresponding to the subway stops - in this case Carlton and Wellesley) began forming. There was, in fact, such a surplus of apartments in this particular area, that landlords 'didn't care who they rented them to', thus paving the way for a 'gay invasion' of sorts. The gay men who settled in the Church-Wellesley area, in its beginnings, were mostly single, which is understandable, considering the historical context: the gay 'community' in the late fifties was, at best, an underground network, as homosexuality was still illegal. Stable, monogamous relationships between men (ie. to the point of 'moving in together') were the exception rather than the rule. Soon thereafter (in fact, almost simultaneously), and somewhat paradoxically, the sixties were a time of sexual liberty, when experimentation and freedom from commitment were a way of life for young people, a way of life which was amplified greatly within the gay community. As a result of these cumulative pressures, unmarried homosexual men tended to live by themselves. The sexual revolution of the sixties also meant that young people began discovering, and affirming, their sexuality at a much younger age than in previous decades. As such, gay men started gaining their independence (sexual and otherwise) in their twenties, rather than in their thirties or beyond. Therefore, the majority of homosexuals who moved in to downtown Toronto in the late fifties and then the sixties were much younger, much more idealistic, much more openly gay than their predecessors. Such demographics and personality traits helped foster the

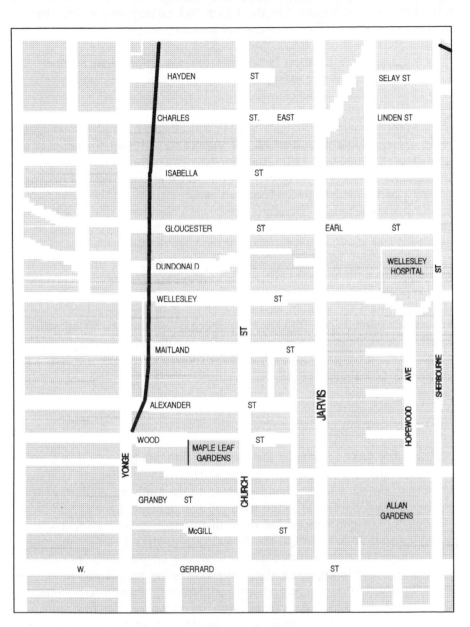

Map of the 'Gay Ghetto', Toronto

development of what today is considered Canada's most sophisticated and outspoken gay community. In the fifties and earlier, as put forth by one long-time member of Toronto's gay community,

> .... gays were diffused throughout the city, [they] had no one focal point, but the focal points were really pinpoints, and they were the bars. (businessman)

These bars, 'beer parlours' and 'hotels' were located mainly along Queen Street West, including a strip on the site of the present Sheraton Hotel, across from Toronto City Hall. And, once the gay population began focusing itself along Church Street between Carlton and Wellesley, the 'scene' began moving east to Yonge Street (Toronto's main 'strip':), and worked its way up north along Yonge, covering, first, the Westbury Hotel (where the basement beer parlour became gay), then the St.Charles Tavern, and so on, northward and eastward until it reached the Church-Wellesley area, where it still thrives today. Homosexual residents, at the time (ie. 1960's and '70's), observed this convergence of gay activities and households, and even foresaw a new 'Castro Street'.

However, such recognition would not come until the early 1980's. And, this paper contends, gentrification by the gay community in an adjacent neighbourhood had much to do with reinforcing the homosexual presence in the area and, thus, with establishing firm roots upon which Toronto's gay community could anchor itself.

The Gentrification of Cabbagetown

Cabbagetown is a rather large inner-city neighbourhood east of downtown Toronto. Bordering on the gay ghetto's eastern-most edge, it is roughly bounded to the west by Sherbourne Street, to the north by Wellesley, to the east by the Don River and to the south by Dundas Street.

Within this neighbourhood are three distinct sub-areas: Regent Park (a public housing project built in the fifties); a considerable area containing a large number of tightly-compacted row-and/or single-family houses, and multi-family dwellings; and a third area containing an eclectic mixture of larger homes (on large properties) and smaller, unassuming homes in concentrated numbers. As can be seen on Figure 2, the first and third sub-neighbourhoods form pods in the larger area of Cabbagetown, with clearly-defined boundaries, boundaries which are equally as visible on the landscape itself as on a map. And it is because of these boundaries (spatial and social) that residents of the third area, wanting to be distinct from

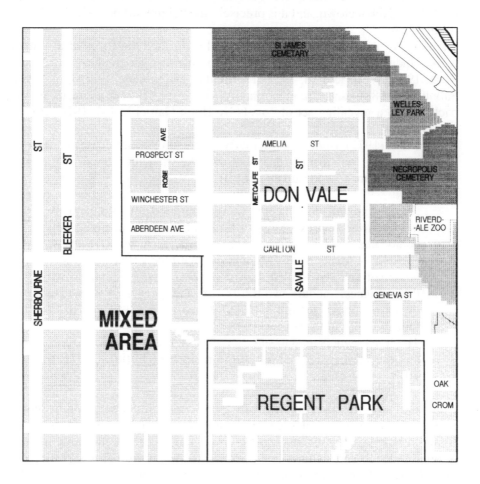

Map of 'Cabbagetown', Toronto.

Cabbagetown and its association with the lower-class area of Regent Park, declared themselves the Don Vale neighbourhood in the late sixties. It is this neighbourhood which we generally speak of when we talk about gentrified Cabbagetown, and it is precisely the neighbourhood which is being studied here.

This is not the first time that Don Vale has formed the focus of a written work. Indeed, it has been the subject of numerous geographic studies (eg. Rose, 1974; Wekerle et al, 1974; Tsimikalis, 1983; Kary, 1988; Ley, 1988; Sabourin, 1988), and an ethnography (Lorimer, 1971), as well as the backdrop to a revealing set of novels by Hugh Garner (1966, 1976, among others).

Lorimer's (1971) work is particularly interesting in this case, because it offers a vivid yet factual snapshot of the neighbourhood as it was immediately prior to widespread gentrification:

> ...a downtown, low-income neighbourhood of old, mostly modest-sized houses. Most of its residents have incomes well below the city's average, and only a very few [...] have above-average incomes. Most men have blue-collar jobs, more unskilled and semiskilled than skilled. Half the families own their homes; about two-thirds of the area's houses are owner-occupied, though some of these have a second tenant family living in them as well.
> The homeowners tend to stay in the same house for a long time, and they form a core of long-time residents.(Lotimer, 1971, p 10)

Garner's (1976) observations correspond to Lorimer's, as he paints a picture of hard-working, blue-collar "mainly manual" (p 22) characters, many living in boarding houses, but most owning single- or shared-family homes. Sabourin (1988) corroborates and documents these informal observations in her study of private renovations in Cabbagetown, describing the neighbourhood as not only typical of urban working-class districts in the late 1960's, but also as an excellent candidate for middle-class re-investment and, thus, gentrification.

Indeed, of the three sub-areas described earlier, Don Vale is the most gentrifiable. Houses there are quite distinctive architecturally (Victorian homes with great architectural detail, some of them considerably large), revealing "a very wide range of sizes and architectural styles" (Lorimer, 1971, p 11), and the neighbourhood boasts a unique urban park (Riverdale Farm), as well as many mature trees along its streets. Garner (1968) describes the area's streets, in the early 1930's, as "lined with single-family houses, many of whose upper stories accommodated a second family" and as being "almost without tenements" (p 6). And Sabourin (1988) notes that

> the most common type of house is a two- or two-and-a-half storey gabled semidetached or row structure [...] built for working class families. (Sabourin, 1988, pp 40-42).

One current resident recalls walking around the neighbourhood on summer evenings, before he lived there, some twenty-five years ago:

> In those days, stained glass was the thing, and there was more stained glass to be had in Cabbagetown than any place I'd ever seen [...] We'd walk up and down the streets and look at these gorgeous homes. My fantasy was to have a home in Cabbagetown. (city politician - Feb. 1992)

Thus, in the late 1960's, over one hundred years after the houses were built, and even though many of the properties were run-down and/or used as rooming houses, the innate quality of the buildings was no less apparent. And, evidently, the potential of these homes did not go unnoticed.

As shown in Fig. 2, Don Vale is the sub-area which is closest to the gay ghetto. It is therefore no coincidence that gays were among the first to discover its potential for gentrification, a fact noted by Garner (1976) when, near the end of his novel, he introduces a flamboyant gay couple as buyers of one of the homes, complete with grand schemes of redecorating and remodelling. In fact, the late Darrell Kent, an influential gay businessman who was to become a prominent real estate agent within the gay community, was among the first to discover the potential of the area and to invest in it, when he and a partner bought a property there in the late 1960's and renovated it (Tsimikalis, 1983). The gay men who had settled the Church-Wellesley area apartments ten to fifteen years earlier were now older, and

> prepared to move into realizing[their] middle-class ideals, which is single-family dwellings in a neighbourhood" (city politician - Feb. 1992)

after having come into their own financially, socially, and otherwise. The 'nesting instinct' was beginning to surface, and Mr. Kent, who had a lot of gay friends and acquaintances, saw this change of attitude and took advantage of it by directing his gay clients to the neighbourhood. As suggested by Castells & Murphy (1982), gay men are opposed to suburban, middle-class ideals in principle, so this urban version of family life was an

73

ideal which they could identify with much more easily as their urge to settle down began to manifest itself:

> Darrell Kent's promotion of Cabbagetown let gay singles and couples know there was an affordable place to go that was neither homogeneous nor suburban. (student/real estate agent -Sept. 1992)

Clearly, most of these clients and realtors realize today that these were not difficult sales: the location, adjacent to the gay ghetto and close to downtown employment, was ideal, and the character of the neighbourhood was one which was easily recognized and appreciated by the prospective buyers. Thus, the first gentrifiers, or 'whitepainters' as they were known in Toronto at the time, moved into Cabbagetown, in the late sixties and early seventies.

Of course, the first gentrifiers were not all gay: Bill Joyce, another pioneer real estate agent in the Cabbagetown area, recalls that only about three of every ten houses he sold was to a gay man or household. However, relative to the gay population at large (estimated to be about 10%), this is a sizable proportion to be concentrated all in one neighbourhood. A landscape architect also remembers a number of the first whitepainters being employees of the Canadian Broadcasting Corporation (CBC), straight and gay, an understandable choice of location considering that many of the CBC's main buildings are located in and around the Church-Wellesley and Cabbagetown areas. Many of the residents today are still employed in the performing arts (radio, television, theatre, etc.), professions which, incidentally, typically attract gays.

As suggested by Sabourin (1988), Tsimikalis (1983) and Kary (1988), the ensuing transformation of the area was translated into increased land and property values. Kary (1988) illustrated these changes by comparing average house prices in the census subdivision containing Cabbagetown to those of Metropolitan Toronto for the years 1965 through to 1984. Graphing these figures (Fig. 3) yields a telling picture, with prices in the area climbing drastically (relative to Metropolitan prices) in the late 1970's, a sure sign that the economic make-up of the area was changing.

In addition, Sabourin's (1988) research indicates that purchasers went from being machinists, mechanics, painters and labourers (in 1955) to being financial analysts, professors, town planners, teachers and musicians (in 1975) (pp.53-54). Such a shift from semiskilled to professional employment is a well-documented symptom of gentrification. Based on these observations, therefore, we can safely conclude that gentrification was well under way by the late 1970's, as presumed in this essay.

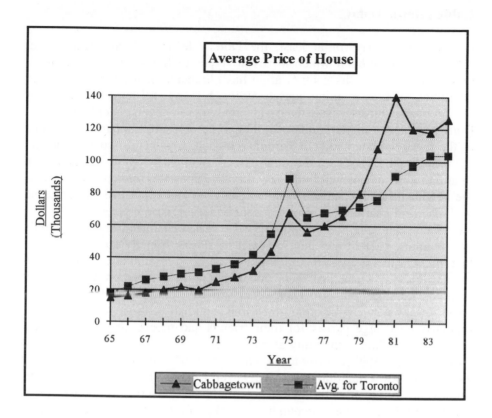

Average Price of House

Dollars (Thousands)

Year

▲ Cabbagetown   ■ Avg. for Toronto

Change in Average Price of Houses in Cabbagetown.

Cabbagetown Today

Cabbagetown today (or at least, the Don Vale area) is an affluent, yet eclectic neighbourhood which mixes all types of households, and houses, rather successfully. Its gentrification has eliminated many multiple-family dwellings, such as rooming houses, although many still remain as the City of Toronto has recently passed a by-law making re-conversion of housing (ie. from multiple- to single-family use) illegal. As a result, Cabbagetown is one of the few neighbourhoods in Toronto - indeed, anywhere - where "you can see winos and BMW's on the same street" (real estate agent - May 1992). In addition, while one will find a few spectacular estates scattered throughout the neighbourhood, complete with coachhouses and expansive gardens, one will also find charming rowhouses, snugly set on narrow lanes.

Residents celebrate the neighbourhood's varied character, and households and families, straight and gay, co-exist in a very friendly atmosphere. In fact, most residents agree that their neighbourhood resembles a small village in many ways, where 'villagers' share not only a common space and a common heritage, but also each other's lives: neighbours here are also friends. Gay men can be quite gregarious, and half of the men I spoke with regularly host large parties for their friends and neighbours, thus keeping alive the close-knit-community atmosphere.

In addition, Cabbagetown has an annual festival, called the Cabbagetown Tour of Homes, a tradition started by Darrell Kent, to showcase these vintage homes and, thus, market the area to potential home-buyers (Tsimikalis,1983). Thus, every Fall, anyone can purchase a ticket and tour a number of the most exquisite homes in the neighbourhood. This event is entirely organized by the residents and, as such, adds to the social agenda of the neighbourhood.

Cabbagetown residents are therefore quite proud of their neighbourhood as a whole. For they value not only their homes (which are indeed valuable), but also the whole concept of what Cabbagetown means: a myriad assortment of individuals, backgrounds, interests and aspirations, all sharing a common respect for, and attachment to, their neighbourhood. And, walking along its streets, one cannot fail to recognize the special character of the surroundings, nor to forget that residents are merely blocks away from the busy, noisy core of Toronto's downtown, not the least of its most distinctive and appealing features.

Repercussions on the Status of the Gay Community in Toronto

The role of gay men in the establishment of such a widely recognized neighbourhood has resulted in a reinforcement of the gay presence in downtown Toronto. Much like Castro Street in San Francisco, the

76

gentrification of Cabbagetown has created a nucleus of sedentary gay households. Homosexuals who choose to settle in downtown Toronto now have a variety of housing types to choose from, a range that includes bachelor apartments, full apartments, condominiums and single-family homes. And, more importantly, the gay life-cycle stages are now all represented and catered to within this area of Toronto - from 'coming out' to settling down in an alternative familial context. This diversity of choices within a relatively small area has allowed homosexuals to remain in the same general area, thus reinforcing the gay identity of the area and giving gay-owned and/or gay-related services a stable market. As a result, Church-Wellesley only really started to be widely recognized by all Torontonians and homosexual Canadians in the early 1980's, over a decade after gays first bought into Cabbagetown. And the area has thrived ever since - enough, evidently, to warrant special recognition by City Hall.

Although many gay men who live in Cabbagetown say they are not involved in the Church-Wellesley 'scene' anymore (ie. since they moved to Cabbagetown), the same men will admit they periodically patronize restaurants or specialty shops there, or use the YMCA facilities in the area. As well, other goods and services which previously found no market in the area now enjoy healthy patronage by this new breed of resident: the mature, settled, even domesticated gay man who needs a butcher, a hardware store and a vegetable market, much like his straight, suburban counterpart. In addition, and more importantly, the presence of such a permanent gay settlement has undeniably served as an attraction for young homosexual men looking for a place to come out and to live, which, in turn, has helped to increase the gay presence, and its associated market, in the Church-Wellesley neighbourhood.

The development of such a foundation for the homosexual community of Toronto has also manifested itself in city politics, as the city's first openly gay councillor, Mr. Kyle Rae, was elected in the fall of 1991 for the ward covering the Church-Wellesley neighbourhood. This achievement is quite significant, especially since it is not the first time an openly gay man has run for office in that ward. Of course, this does not mean that Mr. Rae was elected solely due to his sexual orientation, nor that all voters were themselves homosexual. Nonetheless, one can safely assume that the demographics and/or attitudes of the neighbourhood have changed since the 1970's (when the first gay candidate ran for council), to the point where the majority of its residents are, apparently, open-minded enough to feel positive about being represented by a homosexual man.

Such a manifest display of gay-positive behaviour and activity is, without a doubt, the result of a solid and significant gay community. And such a community, I contend, is itself a direct result of the settlement and gentrification of Cabbagetown by homosexuals.

The Gentrification of Riverdale

Riverdale is the new locale for contemporary gay gentrification. Cabbagetown reached its potential long ago, and today's homosexual singles and couples, themselves feeling the 'urge to nest', have had to reach further to find adequate housing stock. Riverdale, east of the Don River which separates it from the eastern border of Cabbagetown, is the current address of the new generation of gentrifying gays. Not only is the character of this neighbourhood vastly different from that of Cabbagetown (see Dantas: 1988), but, perhaps more importantly, this new generation of young gay households is quite different from that of the men who pioneered the gentrification of Toronto in the seventies.

Unlike Cabbagetown, Riverdale "would not, according to the literature on the topic, be expected to attract gentrifying-minded households" (Dantas, 1988, 75). Rather, the neighbourhood possesses an ethnic heritage and "plain and unassuming" (Dantas, 1988, 74) housing stock, which are not typical of gentrifiable neighbourhoods. The houses are still interesting in that they are an antithesis to the pre-fabricated 'box-homes' of the modern suburbs, though they are considerably more humble than some of their Cabbagetown counterparts. As shown by Dantas (1988) however, and as evidenced by touring Riverdale, the neighbourhood is indeed undergoing gentrification. Gentrifiers there have seemingly succeeded in improving the appearance and value of these homes, much in the same proportions as their predecessors in Cabbagetown, but for vastly differing reasons.

The younger generation which is involved in the gentrification of Riverdale comprises individuals who have developed significantly, even since the emancipated gay men of the seventies. The majority of young gay men today, unlike those of twenty years ago, accept their sexuality in a way which is much less rebellious, much more, in their own words, "gay-positive".

They do not seek to make bold statements, nor do they try to shock with their behaviour. The prevailing philosophy is one of personal acceptance and well-being: the self-destructive lifestyle of years past, caused by deeply-rooted feelings of worthlessness and alienation (see the work of Altman, 1982), is being rejected by this generation, which was raised to feel more positive and open about itself.

Certainly, today's homosexual youth still seeks areas such as the ghetto in the initial stages of his gay life (see Castells & Murphy, 1982; Davis, 1992; Levine, 1979; and Lauria & Knopp, 1985 among others). However, once homosexual men proceed through their various life stages, they strive to rise above the extrovert lifestyle offered by the ghetto, and settle in a neighbourhood which is more acceptable to their new life-style requirements.

By contrast, the Cabbagetown gentrifiers, as testified to in personal interviews, seem to have an implicit attachment to the ghetto - perhaps because of its historical significance to them as a community and, thus, they initially sought to settle in a location which was close to this symbol of their identity.

Thus, to the modern gay gentrifiers, proximity to the ghetto was not a priority in selecting their new homes - if anything, the ghetto became a "push" factor. Instead, proximity to their spiritual centre (the Metropolitan Community Church is located in Riverdale) and to an interesting Toronto neighbourhood (the Danforth strip) seemed much more meaningful motivations. Undoubtedly, financial potential and cheap housing were equally, if not more, of an incentive. However, artificial "belonging" and "tradition", if solely reflected in the neighbourhood's historical and social context (which, in the case of Riverdale, does not come close to Cabbagetown's) was apparently not an issue either. Clearly, gay men today feel enough of a sense of self-worth, tradition and belonging in themselves, that their housing can truly become a reflection of themselves, and not a statement of their wanting to overcome their marginality.

As a result, gay gentrification in Riverdale is much more low-key, and more oriented towards interior remodelling, as opposed to exterior refacing. Image is not as much of an issue here as it was (and still is) in Cabbagetown. The main priority is to create a home, to be enjoyed by the couple and their friends, not to put up a facade which, in the words of one lesbian woman, "screams 'gay-owned'" (public servant - Feb. 1992).

Conclusion

As in most other such instances, the contribution made by the gay community in Toronto has not been given its due regard. Indeed, city officials are either unaware of the homosexual presence in Cabbagetown, or refuse to acknowledge it. In the Church-Wellesley area, in the course of the "Cityplan 91" official plan review, consultants could only observe the "unusually high number of single-male households" (city politician - August 1991). In this case, this veiled comment was particularly noted since one of the planning committee members in the audience was Mr. Kyle Rae, at the time administrator of the 519 Community Centre. Planners, therefore, need to see and recognize the salient characteristics of the population they deal with, and respond to their needs accordingly. Planning theory too often focuses on process, ignoring the character of local communities. Nonetheless, planning must, in the end, benefit people and, thus, must integrate their individual needs. Traditional, normative planning models are no longer adequate for today's communities (if, indeed, they ever were), and alternative models, such as Dykeman's (1992) 'self-help' model, or perhaps even a co-management approach to community planning, must be developed and encouraged. Finally, this population diversity must be recognized for what it is: an important factor in creating the vibrant inner cities which we, as urbanists, value, and which visitors to our cities expect and appreciate.

Thus, as evidenced by this and other case studies (Castells & Murphy, 1982; Pattison, 1983), gay communities have had, and continue to have, influence over how their territory is managed. It is up to planners and other city officials to recognize this valuable population, and harness this potential energy in the interest of furthering community planning efforts. If it is true that community members will become more and more significant allies in neighbourhood planning, then perhaps the gay community - which has until now largely been regarded as no more than a freak-like, fringe population - should be considered more seriously and utilized to its full potential. Clearly, this is feasible, and desirable, in terms of their economic influence as gentrifiers, as well as their political influence, as a highly politically-oriented community.

Bibliography

Adam, B.D. (1978) *The Survival of Domination*, Elsevier North-Holland Inc, New York.

Altman, D. (1982) *The Homosexualization of America*, Beacon Press, Beacon Press.

Blacke-Fraser, A., R. Frank, S. Horvath, L. Kitchen, J. Oh, and S. Steinberg. (1991) *Ethnic-Like Characteristics of the Toronto Lesbian and Gay Community*, Paper written for Dr. Dennis Magill's Sociology 369A course. Copy available from Dr. Magill at University of Toronto upon request.

Blumenfeld, W.J., and D. Raymond. (1988) *Looking at Gay and Lesbian Life*, Beacon Press, Boston.

Bouthillette, A.-M. (1992) *The Role of Gay Communities in the Gentrification of Inner Cities*, Undergraduate thesis submitted to the School of Urban and Regional Planning, University of Waterloo, Waterloo, Ontario, Canada. Available on microfiche from the School.

Breton, R. (1964) "Institutional completeness of ethnic communities and the personal relations of immigrants". *American Journal of Sociology*, 70(2), pp 193-205.

Breton, R., W.W. Isajiw, W.E. Kalbach and J.G. Reitz. (1990) *Ethnic Identity and Equality*, Toronto: University of Toronto Press.

Castells, M. (1983) *The City and the Grassroots*, University of California Press, Berkeley.

Castells, M. and K. Murphy. (1982) "Cultural identity and urban structure: the spatial organization of San Francisco's gay community", Fainstein, N. and Fainstein, S. (eds)*Urban Policy Under Capitalism*, Sage, Beverley Hills.

Clay, P. (1979) *Neighbourhood Renewal*, Lexington Books, Lexington.

Dantas, A. (1988) "Overspill as an alternative style of gentrification: the case of Riverdale, Toronto"., Bunting, T.E., Filion, P. (eds) *The Changing Canadian Inner City*, University of Waterloo, Department of Geography, Ontario.

Davidoff, L., L'Esperance, J. and Newby, H. (1976) "Landscape with Figures: Home and Community in English Society". Mitchell, J. and Oakley, A. (eds) *The Rights and Wrongs of Women*, pp 139-175. Penguin, Harmondsworth.

Davis, T. (1992) *Social processes and political activism: alternative lesbian and gay spatial strategies for social change*, Paper presented at the Annual Meeting of the Association of American Geographers, San Diego, CA, 20 April 1992. Copy available from the author at Clark University.

Dykeman, F. (1992) "Leadership and Community Renewal: Exploring the Planner's Role", *Plan Canada*, Sept., pp 7-11.

Harry, J., DeVall, W.B. (1978) *The Social Organization of Gay Males*, Praeger, New York.

Kary, K.J. (1988) "The gentrification of Toronto and the rent gap theory", Bunting, T.E., Filion, P. (eds) *The Changing Canadian Inner City*, University of Waterloo, Department of Geography, Waterloo, Ont

Lauria, M., Knopp, L. (1985) "Towards an analysis of the role of gay communities in the urban renaissance". *Urban Geography*, 6 (2), pp 152-169.

Levine, M. (1979) "Gay Ghetto", *Journal of Homosexuality*, 4, pp 363-377.

Ley, D. (1988) "Social Upgrading in Six Canadian Inner Cities". *The Canadian Geographer*, 32, pp 31-45.

Moore Milroy, B. (1991a) "People, Urban Space and Advantage", Bunting, T.E., Filion, P. (eds) *Canadian Cities in Transition*, Oxford University Press, Toronto.

Moore Milroy, B. (1991b). "Taking Stock of Planning, Space, and Gender". *Journal of Planning Literature*, 6(1), pp 3-15.

Murray, S.O. (1979) "The institutional elaboration of a quasi-ethnic community". *International Review of Modern Sociology*, 9, pp 165-178.

Pattison, T. (1983) "The stages of gentrification: the case of Bay Village". Clay, P., Hollister, R.M. (eds) *Neighborhood Policy and Planning*, Lexington Press, Lexinton, Mass.

Rose, A. (1974) *Citizen Participation in Urban Renewal*, University of Toronto, Centre for Urban and Community Studies, Toronto.

Rose, D. (1984). "Rethinking Gentrification: Beyond the Uneven Development of Marxist Urban Theory". *Environment and Planning D: Society and Space*, 1, pp 47-74.

Rose, D. (1989) "A Feminist Perspective on Employment Restructuring and Gentrification: the Case of Montreal", Wolch, J., Dear, M., (eds) *The Power of Geography: How Territory Shapes Social Life*, Unwin Hyman, Boston.

Sabourin, J. (1988) *The Process of Gentrification: The Example of Private Housing Renovation in Don Vale, Toronto*, York University, PhD Dissertation, Toronto.

Tsimikalis, S. (1983) *The Gentrification of Don Vale: the Role of the Realtor*, York University, Faculty of Environmental Studies, B.A. thesis, Toronto

Warren, Carol B., (1978) *Identity and Community in the Gay World*. John Wiley & Sons, New York.

Wekerle, G. et al. (1974) *New from Old: A Pilot Study of Housing Rehabilitation and Neighbourhood Change*, Central Mortgage and Housing Corporation, Ottowa.

Winchester, H.P.M., White, P.E., (1988) "The location of marginalised groups in the inner city", *Environment and Planning D: Society and Space*, 6, pp 37-54.

Yeates, M. (1990) *The North American City*, 4th edition, Harper & Row, Publishers, New York.

5 A sociological pub crawl around gay Newcastle

Marc Lewis

Newcastle: Always on the Margins

The Commercial gay scene of Newcastle upon Tyne is not only cultural and spatially marginal to the mainstream life of the city but it also takes place in a conurbation which can be said to be marginal to the British socio-economic system as a whole. The four Tyneside metropolitan boroughs of Newcastle, Gateshead, North Tyneside and South Tyneside have a declining population level of just below a million, the lowest of the major English conurbations. Tyneside is physically isolated in North East England being some 430km distant from London, 160km from Leeds and 200km from Edinburgh. It is also psychological isolated from national social trends in that a majority of the region's people demonstrate a tenacious working class culture. As Byrne (1992 in Colls and Lancaster, 1992, p.35) comments "it is easy to identify the overwhelmingly collectivist and socialist objectives of the people of the Northern region", interestingly these social priorities are not confined to the working class. Lancaster (1992 in Colls and Lancaster, 1992, p 65) observes "if we poke and probe the thicker of the middle-class Newcastle we are struck by the degree of cultural identity that it shares with the working class". Accordingly Tyneside is also politically marginalised by the current rightist tendency of English politics.

This process of isolation and marginalisation is further reinforced by the decline of the region's industrial base which has been greatly exacerbated by the 'free market' policies followed by national government since 1979. Between 1978 and 1984 alone employment in manufacturing industries in the conurbation fell by 46% (Robinson 1988, p.46-47). In common with the national pattern, service industries have become predominant often accompanied by the casualisation, part-time work, and low wages which appear to be an increasing feature of this sector. The near destruction of the region's traditional industrial base of coal mining, shipbuilding, armaments and other heavy industries has resulted in a disturbingly high level of

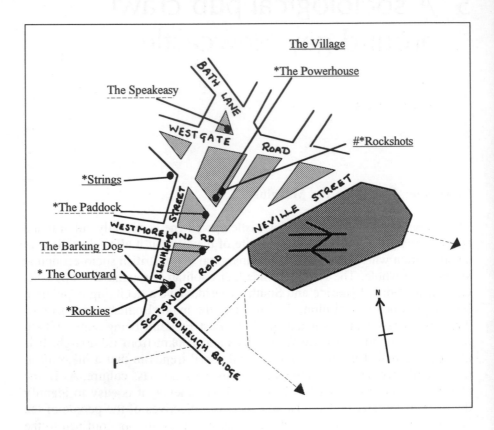

The Village

*The Powerhouse

The Speakeasy

BATH LANE

WESTGATE ROAD

#*Rockshots

*Strings

BLENHEIM STREET

NEVILLE STREET

*The Paddock

WESTMORELAND RD

The Barking Dog

* The Courtyard

*Rockies

SCOTSWOOD ROAD

REDHEUGH BRIDGE

N

Key:

*	Listed in Gay Times "Round Britain Gay Guide"
————	All Gay establishment
- - - - - - - -	Mixed (Gay/Straight) establishment
#	Nightclub

The Commercial Gay Scene in Newcastle Upon Tyne

structural unemployment in parts of Tyneside and subcultures based on crime and the black economy are emerging which are alienated from generally accepted social norms.

However, this picture of industrial decline, unemployment and deprivation is belied by Newcastle's impressive neo-classical city centre with its well patronised shops, restaurants, theatres, cinemas and art gallery. The heart of Tyneside *at Monument* is linked to the outlying areas by the clean, efficient and modern metro rapid transit system. A visitor to the city watching the Saturday shoppers stream out of the central underground stations might conclude that all is fundamentally well. Certainly for the majority of the population who are in work and who have inexpensive and good housing. This along with the still surviving legacy of good public services, allows the relatively high levels of discretionary spending as witnessed by Newcastle's vibrant and famed night-life. This culture of instant gratification needs to be seen in the context of a traditionally fragile local labour market dependent in the past on the waxing and wearing of the fortunes of heavy industry. Today employment is based heavily on routine administration in the public sector together with the service industries. For many Tyneside employees in both the working and middle classes there is an acute awareness that a political or commercial decision taken in London could deprive them of their jobs tomorrow, and that only one pay cheque separates them from unemployment and relative poverty. This constant sense of insecurity, of living in a region with a 'branch economy', explains the well documented Geordie tendency to 'live for today and let tomorrow take care of itself'.

The distinct cultural tradition of the North-East has resulted in the continuing dominance of attitudes to socio-sexual roles that have been considerably eroded elsewhere. For the North-Eastern heterosexual man 'work' is the prerogative of the male and employment by women continues to be subsidiary to their true raison d'etre of housework and 'looking after us bairns'. The belief that 'work' consists of backbreaking heavy industrial labour carried out by heavy drinking, muscular, 'real men' in a social atmosphere of strong male bonding continues to persist despite the reality of de-industrialisation and the feminisation of the workforce. It is no surprise that this machismo culture is replete with a contempt for feminist values and inevitably for 'them poofs'. Together with persisting heterosexual stereotypes also survives that of the effeminate gay man. Whereas in London a leather-clad clone travelling on the Underground would be readily identified by many other travellers as being a gay man, commuters on Tyneside would be more likely to dismiss him as a biker on the way to collect his machine!

Such general lack of awareness of the reality of gay culture does have advantages in that members of the community go relatively unmolested (although any streetwise Geordie knows where the gay venues are). However the 'effeminate gay' stereotype does seem to present a major problem for many men in coming to terms with their sexuality in that they are unable to identify with the stereotype and are unaware of other ways of being gay. This ontological conflict, together with community pressures to conform, may explain why working class gays are relatively under-represented on the Newcastle scene which as Pronger (1990, p 7) notes displays "considerable bias towards *acculturation*, some degree of overtness, and a higher educational and socio-economic level." Nevertheless Newcastle's gay scene does have a decidedly working class character compared to other major British cities. Working class gays and lesbians who have 'come out' frequently have stories to tell of rejection or animosity by their families and sometimes of virulent persecution by neighbours. This is particularly true of people living on some of the area's public having estates - in the case of Newcastle's Cruddas Park Estate the authorities have found it necessary to establish programmes in an attempt to counteract homophobia and racism.

Although the exact position is difficult to quantify through talking to regular habitues of the scene one gets the distinct impression that many working class gay and lesbian young people continue to be forced into marriage by the strength of social convention. Certainly rather more than usual men and women on the city's scene are or have been married which indicates that conditions for gays and lesbians are decidedly hostile at some levels of Tyneside's social strata. The contribution of lesbians to Newcastle's gay scene is a high-profile one, however, the rest of this paper relates mainly to the region's gay male population. This is not to suggest that the experience of Tyneside lesbians is either unimportant or inconsequential but simply that there are those better qualified to discuss their approach to the business of being homosexual.

A social setting like that of Tyneside in which the gay community is firmly marginalised requires the development of a different physical and psychological symbolic world so that a separate cultural identity can be created and maintained amongst gay men. Plummer discusses the psychological aspects of such symbolism.

> Central to any comprehension of the homosexual subculture, indeed the central element, is the existence of a quite distinctive perception of the world. To put it simply: male homosexuals are 'boy' watchers. In contrast and as simply, male heterosexuals are 'girl' watchers. No comprehension of the homosexual world is possible unless this point is grasped. Such a puritan distinction means of course that people in the homosexual subculture regularly and routinely apprehend other men as erotic objects : at work, watching television, walking along the street, at parties, in moments of 'time out' and reverie, the young man's fancy turns to other men. It is the world of the waking

heterosexual man in reverse - with all the variations in kinds of objects and intensity of attraction that this implies. (Plummer, 1975, p 158-9)

Of course it is precisely these symbolic variations as described by Plummer that enabled the gay community to function as a hidden 'demi-monde' before the 1967 Sexual Offences Act, and which still operates as a shared world of distinct meaning today. Even when the heterosexual community has invitingly adopted the physical manifestations of gay symbolism (such as earrings worn by men, the wearing of keys from the jeans belt or the 'clone look' - all much in evidence amongst the straight men of Tyneside) there remains more than ample culturally differentiated common ground for two gay men meeting outside the scene, say on a work related occasion, to be able to test each other in order to determine the other's sexual orientation. Such tentative communication might be initiated by eye-contact and if successful then perhaps proceed to a discussion of favourite pubs, or a mention of a well known 'cruising ground'.

In the larger cities, but not Newcastle, an individual's regular bar not only identifies them as being gay but to those 'in the know' will also indicate membership of one of the subcultures within the community.

In this context Newcastle's Hanover Gardens, London's Hampstead Heath or Edinburgh's Warriston cemetery take on a set of meetings and significance far removed from their usual amenity or botanical reputation! Thus the different symbolic world of the gay man not only serves to create a cohesive community within the gay domain, through the agency of a shared perception of the erotic world and the development of alternative symbolism and common characteristics, but it also allows gays to identify and sustain each other (rather in the nature of a socio-sexual fifth column) in heterosexual society. The necessity for a discrete symbolic system is a strong indication of social marginality but participation in such a system also suggests a level of accultivation.

For those who for various reasons are unwilling to frequent the gay commercial scene, cruising grounds will often be the first point of contact with other men. Ironically although a campaign against the use of Hanover Gardens for cruising by a Newcastle newspaper initially led to a dramatic increase in 'queer-bashing' in the area, it also resulted in many men who were previously oblivious of its existence using it to indulge in gay sexual activity. Some of these 'new recruits' have graduated to become members of the commercial scene subculture although many remain married and merely 'dabble' at the periphery of the gay community.

Pub Crawling

The gay scene of Newcastle is geographically compact and contained within streets not more than ½km from the North West to the South West of the central railway station. The area is best described as being predominantly non-residential inner-city apart from a large block of housing association flats on Waterloo Street, many residents of which are gay. This area to the west of the city centre is spatially marginal being occupied by a number of large car parks, railway land and small businesses. It has a rundown and neglected but comfortable atmosphere. There is easy access through good public transport links to the rest of Tyneside and the Northern region and as mentioned there is ample off-peak parking. The catchment of the Newcastle scene is huge, extending from the Scottish border at Berwick in the north, to Carlisle in the west, and down to Teeside and North Yorkshire in the South. In general Newcastle's 'gay village' is a fairly safe territory, the main roads in the area being wide and well lit, and the majority of heterosexual pubs and clubs from which trouble of a homophobic nature could originate being to the east in the city centre. The Gay Times "Round Britain Gay Guide" for July 1991 which was current at the time of the research listed six different venues in the area, of which four were pubs and two were nightclubs. In addition there is one new all-gay bar and two 'mixed' gay/heterosexual bars not listed in the guide.

Starting on the Scotswood Road, "The Courtyard" is the longest established gay pub in the city having been opened in the early 1980's. As its name would suggest, the interior decor represents a mediterranean courtyard with a well in the centre. The clientele of The Courtyard tends to have a greater age, socio-economic and subcultural mix than the other bars. As one customer told me:

> It can be quite good in here at times but sometimes it resembles
> a gay Salvation Army hostel with beer.

Certainly the average age of "Courtyard" customers is older than in general on the Newcastle scene but this is probably accounted for by the establishment's role as a community pub rather than a 'cruising' bar. Although The Courtyard has a juke-box, it is not operated at levels which make conversation impossible, as if often the case on the Newcastle scene, and this is probably an additional attraction to older customers. The pub staff are well established and clearly have a good rapport with their regular customers who also have fairly long-standing acquaintance/friendship bonds amongst themselves. To emphasise The Courtyard's eclectic clientele mix, on a Wednesday evening in September 1991 customers included a couple of the local 'rent-boys' (male prostitutes), regular customers from Tyneside, some less regular customers from the surrounding region (mainly Wearside, Durham and the Darlington area), the local men's leather club M.S.C. North-East having their bi-weekly social evening, a small group of local lesbians and two gay men from London and Liverpool attending an archivist's conference at Newcastle University. It should be mentioned that of the local regular customers one was wheelchair-bound, and deaf men are regulars. The presence of the disabled at The Courtyard appears to be unusually high in contrast with most gay 'watering holes' where a premium is often put upon physical perfection. The various groups and cliques present were not ignoring each other and there was a fair amount of to-ing and fro-ing between each. The general atmosphere was of sociability and there was no evidence of any sexual behaviour.

Further along the Scotswood Road at its junction with Blenheim Street is "Rockies" which styles itself as a disco bar. Rockies occupies a triangular site and is divided into three different levels containing the bar, a small stage and a dance floor; a lounge/standing area; and a pool table. The atmosphere here is quite different compared to The Courtyard. Decor is what might be characterised as being 'transatlantic plush' and there are a number of television monitors suspended from the ceiling which simultaneously show 'pop' videos. The customers here tend to range in age from their early 20's to late 40's and more consciously display evidence of the gay subcultures alluded to previously in this paper. The mainly male clientele often sport the closely cropped hair and moustache of the classic clone. The clone originated in the United States during the heady days of gay liberation in the 1970's and was in many ways an ironic parody of the archetypal homophobic blue collar worker. Segal notes how at first sight

> This 'butch shift' - gay muscle men clad exclusively in leather and denim, or gay clones; with short hair, moustache, check shirt, blue jeans and 'bovver' boots - would appear to be a celebration of conventional masculinity, just as the reality of much of the sexuality of gay men seems to be an exaggeration of the more promiscuous, emotionally detached, entirely phallocentric encounters characteristics of male heterosexuality. It is now a commonplace perception that gay men have more in common with straight men than with gay women, and vice versa. Gay machismo is, however, defended by many gay men as a new form of camp - the super-macho style exposing the absurdity of masculinity more effectively than effeminacy. (Segal, 1990, p 149)

To an extent the 'butch zone' within the gay community appears to be exclusive and apart from the rest of the gay world. Certainly many participants on the 'general' scene regard it with a mixture of fascination, fear and repulsion. I would suggest that this suspicion is based on an inaccurate understanding of the dynamics of friendship and sex within the network of leather, denim, uniform and/or sadomasochism gays.

There is considerable evidence that macho gays face not only harassment from the agencies of the state but also stigmatisation from other homosexuals. Pickering (1992, p 32) instances the hostile attitude of many political activities at the now defined London Lesbian and Gay Centre towards the "leather and S.M. brigade", whilst in a letter to the weekly paper Capital Gay, Dressen (1992,p 2) equates "the S & M and other fetish scenes "with" the fascism within". The American writer Thompson (1991, p.xii) comments that "Leatherfolk have suffered a long history of harassment, often by other gay people". It may be that this 'internal marginalisation' is based on the suspicion that macho gays are intent on importing the 'bacillus' of dominant heterosexual values into the gay milieu, however, Roberts (1990 in Segal, 1990, p 150) reports an interview with a leather guy into sadomasochism (and it should be stressed that the connection between the two is not automatic) which give a rather different perspective than might be expressed.

> Macho amongst straight men tends to mean they watch "Match of the Day", drink beer, spill pizza on the carpet, treat their wives like ratbags. Now that doesn't interest me at all ..... macho to me, I suppose, means a certain self-assurance ... I like coolness and strength.

Roberts' interviewee goes on to explain that the gay macho lifestyle has not however imported the stunted emotional behaviour of its heterosexual counterpart. He claims, of gay sadomasochists,:

> We're not as competitive. It's almost like a sisterly relationship that women have, you can talk about everything and you'll always be friends.

Another possibility for peer group suspicion of the 'super butch' is their supposed adherence to right wing political views. However a straw poll at a meeting of M.S.C. North-East found a preponderance of Labour Party supporters whilst an official of the uniform club "The London Blues" described the political affiliations of his members as being:

> .... mainstream, certainly no extreme right-wing or anything like that.

92

It will be seen that gays are no less susceptible to the process of labelling and stigmatising minority groups than are heterosexuals. This process is not so surprising given the suggestion by Aggleton and Wilton that:

> People 'make sense' of new ideas they encounter by assessing them in the light of pre-existing beliefs, interpreting them accordingly, and fitting them in with what they already know. (Aggleton and Wilton, 1991, in Aggleton et al 1991, p 149)

Since the dominant value system stigmatises variant sexual practices as being socially and, as in the case of sadomasochism, politically suspect there is an inevitability that this process should be replicated within the gay and lesbian communities as well as being used against them. As far as macho gays are concerned, a connection with dominant male heterosexual values, authoritarian, exploitative and misogynistic attitudes and right-wing political affiliations have arisen in the minds of many other gays who judge the macho subculture on its superficial appearance. As in many areas, Tyneside is also marginal to this subculture and members resident in the region can often be seen in greater numbers in the macho bars of Blackpool, Manchester and London than on the Newcastle scene.

Rockies is certainly one of the Newcastle venues where music can be played at almost deafening levels. The bar employs a disc jockey who appears to increase the volume as the number of customers rises, consequently at busy times attempts at conversation are almost useless and the clientele must direct their attention to consuming alcohol (an uncharitable observer might conclude this is a deliberate tactic by the management to increase sales!), reverie or to cruising. On quieter nights the level of sexually orientated behaviour at Rockies is similar to The Courtyard, that is to say minimal. On such nights customers will usually consist of the small group of men and women who cluster around the pool table to play and to socialise. However at busier times such as weekends and public holidays the bar will be packed with men either dressed in one of the subculture 'uniforms' or expensive fashionable clothing. Rockies tends to be the haunt of younger gay men with a fair amount of disposable income. Many are members of the 'salariat' or small scale entrepreneurs for example. When the pub is busy, evidence of sexually directed behaviour is more plentiful. This behaviour almost invariably consists of three main components: firstly, eye contact is held for a substantial period with the selected partner, often the facial expression will be intense and unsmiling until both parties are sure that they have 'scored' with each other. Secondly, the body posture of the parties involved will be indicative of sexual availability. A man will stand to his full height with his chest expanded out and his stomach pulled in, often one leg will be bent slightly behind him in order to accentuate the crotch. Thirdly, the hands will also be positioned in order to emphasise the lower body either by fitting the thumbs into the jeans belt loops, by grasping the belt or by looping the thumbs into the jeans fronts pockets and allowing the hands to dangle on either side of the crotch. Often verbal communication will be minimal, indeed I have heard of instances where sex has followed the cruising procedure without a single word being exchanged by either participant.

The interesting feature about cruising is not so much the techniques which are employed, which could be said to be unimaginative and banal, but in the length of time that it will often occupy. Cruising is not just a form of sexual entrée, it is also a form of speechless communication (albeit somewhat selective!) which lends itself to the noise of bars and discos. Furthermore it is a central fact of life in the gay community. Given that for many gay men sex is seen as an ubiquitous social activity then cruising behaviour is an occupation that will loom fairly large in their lives, the symbolic variations that arise from it have become embedded in the culture of the community. Cruising is not of course always successful. One is reminded of an American cartoon in which two aggrieved looking gays are telling a third handsome but aloof man: "We've both been cruising you for two hours and we just decided to come over and tell you that you're not worth it". Nevertheless it is always a common point of reference and anecdote amongst gay men. In conversation the opinion was fairly frequently expressed that the hunt is often better than the kill to the extent that a fantasy image could be built up of the 'cruisee' over the course of an evening that actual contact could dispel completely. However the general opinion seemed to be that in such circumstances sexual pragmatism would usually win out.

Sexual activity is very important in gay relationship networks because encounters which initially start out with a purely sexual motivation often turn into long-standing warm and supportive friendships. It is not unusual to find men who have made a majority of their friendships in this way. Norris and Read suggest

> In the gay world, where incest and other taboos do not hold sway, friends become lovers and lovers become friends with a speed and ease that may well amaze the heterosexual onlooker, who's sociosexual behaviour is much more curtailed. It is quite common for the social circle of gay men and women to be made up in part of people with whom they have, at one time or another, had a sexual relationship, as if homosexuals are bound to each other by sex, love and friendship, in place of blood. (Morris, Read, 1985, p 175)

The cruising ethos on the scene is a major factor in facilitating such friend/lover networks which may well extend between cities or even internationally.

Unfortunately Tyneside has not been marginalised in the spread of HIV infection and AIDS, although the numbers affected are fewer than in the larger cities. Newcastle bars have their racks of safer sex literature and free condoms and the towns nightclubs hold occasional benefits for AIDS charities. However there appears to be less understanding of the importance and urgency of safer sex practices than in centres such as London and Manchester where men are personally affected by the illness or friends and/or partners. Certainly over the past few years AIDS has changed from being the Newcastle scene's great unmentionable subject to an acknowledged fact of life but because of the region's isolation one suspects that the feeling is quite widespread that HIV infection is something contracted 'out there' rather than on home ground. Another concern is that the safer sex message fails to reach those of the periphery of the scene - those who are nominally 'heterosexual' but who indulge in homosexual activity from time to time. Even amongst acculturated gays on Tyneside the idea of fixed sexual roles, the fucker/fuckee dichotomy, persists. Since research points towards unsafe sex being more likely in fixed role rather than reciprocal sessions a change in this structuring of sexual roles would be desirable (Davies & Weatherburn, 1991 in Aggleton et al 1991, p 123). Nevertheless despite these concerns sexual conduct on the Newcastle scene and the cruising grounds has been modified to some extent by the fear of AIDS. The big question is whether or not the region will mirror the infection levels of the larger conurbations in a few years time.

It is not intended that this brief description of the Newcastle scene should be a tedious catalogue of each licensed premises; rather the intention is to indicate the variety that can be found in one fairly small city. Whilst reference has been made to those who are readily identifiable with one of the gay subcultures it should be stressed that these men are in a minority. In one of the larger cities such as London or Manchester the discrete groups will patronise their own bars and clubs and not mix to any great extent with what might be termed the 'general' gay community. However in Newcastle there is an unusual amount of intermixing not only between the men but also with lesbians. This coexistence is best exemplified at "Strings" on Blenheim Street. The bar is something of an amalgamation of The Courtyard and Rockies. Downstairs the young and fashionable of both sexes drink in a bar decorated in typical 1980's style to the accompaniment of very loud disco music, while upstairs the atmosphere is rather more conductive to conversation and socialising - or a quiet game of pool. Lest it be thought that the scene only functions during the evenings it should be explained that Strings opens from Monday to Saturday at 1400 and remains open until 'last orders' at 2300, with a reduced opening period on Sunday. The Courtyard also has lunch-time opening and afternoon drinkers will often visit Strings after going to The Courtyard. Afternoon sessions in Newcastle probably show the scene at its most friendly and relaxed, visitors to the city will often be drawn into conversation and tipped off about places to visit. In the afternoon the sexual tension and posturing which can be found at night is much less marked.

Newcastle's two gay nightclubs are situated in a large ex-cinema on Waterloo Street, a few minutes walk away from Strings. The longest established of these is owned by Adrian Gadd, the city's largest gay entrepreneur, who also owns The Courtyard and Rockies. "Rockshots" was for many years Newcastle's most popular venue with its two large bars, a dance floor, a quieter area, fast food outlet and a shop selling soft pornography, bottles of 'poppers' (amyl-nitrate, a sexual stimulant), fetish and fashion clothing, etc. Whilst Gadd provided a signal service to the gay community in providing a choice of different venues during the 1980's, it could be argued that his enterprises eventually exploited his monopoly position on the scene. Norris and Read emphasise that

> Gay people tend to be sensitive about the money charged for admission and drinks, because for them, their pubs and clubs are not only places where they go to have a good time, but also often the only places, apart from their own homes, where they can relax with their friends and meet other gay people, in an environment free from heterosexual curiosity and hostility; to pay for the privilege is to add insult to in injury. (Morris, Read, 1985, p 208)

As has been mentioned gay men, not usually having to bear the expense of bringing up children, tend to have larger disposable incomes than do their heterosexual counterparts. However this does not mean that value for money is not looked for in excursions onto the scene, bearing in mind the fact that the prices charged are somewhat higher than in comparable heterosexual establishments in any case. The opening of Mary Ord's "Strings" bar was widely welcomed, not only as an extension of the choice available but also as a challenge to the Gadd monopoly. A price war between the competing businesses duly ensued, only eventually to end up with a small differential between the prices being charged. Waterloo Street's other nightclub "The Powerhouse" is a new venue owned by Philip Reay who returned from Manchester, where he has been involved in nightclub management on that city's highly rated gay scene, to open a rival to Gadd's "Rockshots". The Powerhouse has had considerable success in making deep inroads in Rockshots' market. There seem to be two main reasons for this, as has been mentioned the question of relative value for money is a sensitive one and even a perceived better deal from an alternative commercial enterprise will cause many gay customers to change their traditional allegiances, if only temporarily. Another factor is that of novelty value. The opening of a new venue frequently causes customers to turn up in droves for the first few weeks and months, usually to the disadvantage of established bars and clubs. However this state of affairs is rarely maintained for very long before equilibrium is found. Nevertheless in the interim the new venue's owner can develop an exaggerated sense of commercial success. In many respects Reay's enterprise is simply a larger version of Rockshots and it is questionable if a scene the size of Newcastle's can provide enough business for two gay nightclubs in the longer term. (As a coda whilst revising this paper for publication in September 1993; Mary Ord has sold Strings, which remains gay, and now lives in the United States. Philip Reay has opened another successful bar "The Village" and both The Powerhouse and Rockshots remain very much in business despite the recession). Gadd appears to be dealing with this problem by orientating his policies increasingly towards the heterosexual student market during the week with forays into the gay market at weekends or on special occasions when he feels that it may be profitable to do so. This sort of policy is more in line with predominantly 'straight' nightclubs which have the occasional 'gay night'. In general the attitude of the Newcastle community towards Rockshots appears to be one of increasingly hostility as a venue which was once seen to be gay territory becomes ever less so. This concern seems to be centred on door policy which even on specifically gay nights results in heterosexual men and women gaining access to the club and leading to fairly widespread perception that 'gay behaviour' in Rockshots is now certainly not as sage as it was hitherto.

This last point highlights the accuracy of Norris and Read's comment about the importance of the scene being "an environment free from heterosexual curiosity and hostility." It is noticeable when observing the behaviour of 'scene regulars' at one of the 'mixed' pubs such as the "Barking Dog" that they are much more guarded than they would be on the scene and one is made to realise the extent to which the necessity of 'passing' in heterosexual society circumscribes the behaviour of gay men. From time to time heterosexual men and women will accidentally enter a gay pub without realising that they have done so, this is something that happens fairly frequently at The Courtyard which appears from the outside to be a very ordinary pub. Normally heterosexuals inadvertently straying into gay territory in this way have one drink and leave fairly quickly. This may be because either their gay customers will tend to exclude them in some way by 'closing ranks' either metaphorically or physically, or because the 'trespassers' sense that the social environment that they have entered does not provide the sort of 'markers' that they would expect to find in a heterosexual establishment. This does not mean that the 'straight' friends of gay men and lesbians are not made welcome on the scene, but as in any social group that welcome is conditional upon compliance with the generally accepted norms of that group. Generally speaking heterosexual women seem to find the company of gay men far more acceptable than do heterosexual males and consequently can be found out on the scene far more commonly. It is of course an accurate commonplace that 'straight' women often relish the freedom from the sexual harassment that they experience in gay pubs and clubs.

It is as true of the scene in Newcastle as in any other British city that, if not conspicuous by their total absence, then members of the ethnic minorities are certainly extremely under-represented in relation to their true percentage of the gay population. Certainly the few men of Afro-Caribbean or Chinese origins out on the Newcastle scene appear to encounter few if any problems with overt racism. This is not to claim that racism does not exist amongst the gay community, however it does rarely seem to assume the levels of viciousness and personal vindictiveness that are apparent in other sections of society - although of course given the gay experience of labelling and discrimination it should not exist at all. Ethnic minority gay men may well be doubtful that they would receive the treatment to which they are entitled at the hands of their white confreres, also the strong emphasis on the consumption of alcohol as a social lubricant will obviously present a strong disincentive to members of various religious persuasions. Prejudice against homosexuality is as much a fact of life amongst some minority communities as it is among the Anglo-Celtic majority population. The footballer Justin Fashanu's revelation that he is gay was attacked in the black community newspaper, "The Voice", which in an editorial comment labelled Fashanu's disclosure as being "pathetic and unforgivable... an affront to the whole black community." Resistance to the stigmatisation of ethnic minority gays by their own communities is growing and in areas with large populations of Asian origin such as West Yorkshire, the West Midlands and London 'bangia' discos take place. The absence of all but very few ethnic minority gays on the Newcastle scene is also a function of the fact that:

> Tyneside is an overwhelmingly white area. This perception, apparent to most visitors from other large English cities, can be supported statistically be reference to the fact that the percentage of persons in private households with 'head of household' born in the New Commonwealth or Pakistan is 0.82 per cent on Tyne and Wear as compared to the national average of 4.2 per cent (Bonnett 1993, p 292).

Whilst given the condition of race relations in contemporary Britain it seems likely that the ethnic minorities in high population areas will continue the trend to develop their own gay scenes, it seems probable that on Tyneside ethnic minority gays will continue to depend on the majority population scene for the foreseeable future.

The place of Newcastle's scene within the context of the national gay scene is also marginal since it is primarily of regional significance. Although venues also exist in Middlesbrough and Sunderland, Newcastle is the only scene accessible within forty-five minutes travelling time from most of the North East. Whilst a night out in Edinburgh or Leeds is just about a viable proposition for those living in the extreme north or south (respectively) of the North East, by and large the Newcastle scene has a captive population. The general sense of isolation described at the beginning of this paper is further reinforced as far as the gay scene is concerned by Newcastle's not being a destination on the scene 'milk round' of London, Brighton, Bournemouth, Birmingham and Manchester. It is also too geographically distant to have much contact with the scenes of Glasgow and Edinburgh. Since Newcastle is rarely an object of gay tourism those outsiders who do visit are either on business trips of various kinds, or those who have emigrated from the region returning to visit their families. Consequently the Newcastle scene has a socially endogamous character and a relative isolation from the rest of the British gay scene, possibly with the exception of members of the macho subculture who are obliged to travel in order to pursue their interests. Accordingly the Newcastle gay scene is not only marginalised within its own larger community, which is also peripheral to the British socio-economic system, but it also occupies a marginal place in the British gay scene.

Bibliography

Aggleton, P., Wilton, T., (1991) "Condoms, Coercion and Control: Heterosexuality and the limits to HIV/AIDS Education", Aggleton, P. et al (eds), *Social Aspects of AIDS*, Falmer Press.

Bonnett, A. (1993) "The Formation of Public Professional Radical Consciousness: The Example of Anti-Racism", *Sociology*, Vol 27, No 2, British Sociological Association.

Byrne, D. (1992) "What Sort of Future?", Colls, R., Lancaster, B. (eds), *Geordies*, Edinburgh University Press.

Dressen, R. (1992) "The Fascism Within", *Capital Gay*, 7/2, No 530.

Lancaster, B. (1992) "Newcastle - Capital of What?", Colls, R., Lancaster, B. (eds), *Geordies*, Edinburgh University Press.

Norris, S., Read, E. (1985) *Out in the Open*, Pan Books.

Pickering, B. (1992) "Double Vision", *The Guardian* 9th Jan.

Plummer, K. (1975) *Sexual Stigma - An Interactionalist Account*, Routledge and Kegan Paul.

Pronger, B., (1990) *The Arena of Masculinity - Sports, Homosexuality and the Meaning of Sex*, Gay Men's Press.

Robinson, F. (1988) "Industrial Structure", Robinson, F. (ed) *Post-Industrial Tyneside*, Newcastle Upon Tyne Libraries and Arts.

Segal, L. (1990) *Slow Motion-Changing Masculinities, Changing Men*, Virago Press.

Thompson, M. (ed) (1991) *Leather Folk*, Alyson Publications.

Part III: Marginal issues

Research into lesbian and gay lifestyles has until recently, been conducted by the hetero-patriarchy of academia. They investigated what to them was a group of people with a specific medico-socio-legal problem. The results of such work were often obtained through 'natural science' methods, and very rarely detailed the actual life experiences of lesbians and gay men. Rather, in retrospect, they have provided insight into the researcher's and society's response to homosexuality either as lifestyle or practice. This scientific research would be looking for 'facts' or 'truths', or 'proofs'. Instead social research can be construed as seeking after "meanings".

The justification for doing this type of research is that knowledge obtained, through the work undertaken here, may not be able to provide generalisations about individuals' experiences, but it can be that it is able to be related to and through. For example, it is not thought that knowledge about Manchester's Gay scene can enable us to generalise about the London scene because of their large differences, but they can be related through a commonality of experience. That enables structures and processes to be understood both at a macro and a micro level, within the systems of the state and through the experience of the individual.

The following four chapters attempt to bring together issues as viewed by individuals, which must become part of our theoretical approach in Lesbian and Gay studies, because for so long the individual has been isolated and voiceless.

Part III: Marginal issues

6 Gayspeak, the linguistic fringe: Bona polari, camp, queerspeak and beyond

Leslie J. Cox and Richard J. Fay

Picture the scene : two Gay men in their mid-thirties meet on the street - they know each other from the scene. Pleasantries over, they continue:

A   Are you off out Saturday night?
B   Nanti 'ambag, perhaps next week.

This exchange, recently overheard in Liverpool, typifies some of the language of some Gay men. By use of a kind of code, the exact reason for the negative reply, lack of money, is clear only to code sharers. The ability to slip in and out of code is one aspect of the distinctive language usage of Gay men. We call this distinctive usage *Gayspeak* although this term has been used to describe the language used by both Gay men and Lesbians. Such code adoption in marginalised Gay culture has been regarded by radicals, especially in America, as a self-ghettoising mentality contributing to the continued supremacy of the white male heterosexual orthodoxy and so maintaining the marginalisation of the Gay community. Because the code apparently acquiesces to "the value system of a racist patriarchal culture, those Gays who use it are engaging in self-oppression" (Stanley, 1975, p 385). Gayspeak becomes, in words attributed to Gay militants (Rogers, 1972, Introduction), "another link in the chain which holds the homosexual enslaved". Rather than conform to the assumptions of mainstream orthodoxy, assumptions enshrined in both the 'standard' language and in Gayspeak, the Gay community should either avoid or reclaim it so that *Queerspeak* replaces *Gayspeak*.

Coates (1993) sees women as a *muted group* (Ardener 1975 and 1978a). Gay culture is in some ways equally muted and this status provides one explanation for Gayspeak's dubious foundation:

... in any society there are dominant modes of expression belonging to the dominant group within that society. If members of a muted group want to be heard, they are required to express

103

themselves in the dominant mode ... in many cultures, muted groups are indeed silenced by rules laid down by the dominant group.(Coates 1993, pp 35-6)

Rogers (1972) argues that Gayspeak, a product of the ghetto, is a secret slang which "leaves outsiders where they usually are", a form of protest "used to deflate the hypocrisy of nice-sounding labels that mean nothing to the people that use them", and an expression of social identity allowing other members to recognise group members. But Gayspeak stereotypes just like mainstream language because

> ... Gay slang was coined, invented, dished, and shrieked by the Gay stereotypes: the flaming faggots, men who look like women, flagrant wrist benders, the women who don't shave their legs, all those who find it difficult to be accepted for what they feel they are even within the pariah Gay subculture. And they stereotype others because they themselves have been labelled offensively: they see all Italian straights as members of the Mafia, and they speak of Yiddeshe mamas with a knowing smirk ... they over-dramatize words to make up for the plainness they find in their own lives ... to them life is a stage ... and the audience constantly clapping for more ... they jeer because they have been mocked; they retaliate with a barrage of their own words which ridicule women, male virility, the sanctity of marriage, everything in life from which they are divorced. (Rogers 1972, Introduction)

We believe that the radical perspective focuses on the negative elements of Gayspeak at the expense of the positive. Certainly, Gayspeak does contain many individual items offensive to other marginalised groups in society: the racism of *dinge queen* for a Gay man with a sexual preference for Asian or Black men and the misogyny inherent in *fish* for women. Since language embodies the values of dominant groups, it needs to be constantly reappraised and redefined so as to reflect the pluralistic nature of human society. But the radical perspective ignores the functions, past and present, of Gayspeak, and fails to recognise the overall value of linguistic space in urban culture (1). By reviewing the history of Gayspeak, and assessing its lexicon, themes, settings, and functions, we hope to highlight its positive features.

Two features of UK Gayspeak are illustrated in the exchange above. First, the word *nanti* meaning no\nothing\I haven't got originates from early Gayspeak, known as **Polari**, prominent in Gay 1950's slang but historically much older. The use of *'ambag* for money illustrates a playful word extension from money to purse to handbag. This wordplay, linguistic clever-ness, or *dishing*, is a highly-regarded seam in contemporary Gay culture, a valuable skill outside the sexual marketplace (Hayes 1976, p 265). The exchange also throws out four key aspects of Gayspeak:

1)its historical origins
2)its current vitality
3)its feminising aspect
4)its functions in Gay culture.

Polari - The historical origins of gayspeak

We are consciously extending the reference of the term Polari beyond a synonymy with Gay 1940/50's slang, a limited view reinforced by the recent Summers Out TV series about Gay life in London between 1940-70 (Channel 4 1993). This programme contains dialogues set throughout this period giving a flavour of Polari. Here is the 1940's dialogue set on a London bus:

A   Vogue us up ducky [give us a cig mate] your mother's a stretcher case [I'm knackered].

B   That's because your mother takes her gin on the drip feed.

A   What was I like in that club?

B   Like Mae West only balder and with bigger tits. How much further have we got to go?

A   A mere powder compact's throw from here [not far from here] heartface   [mate] ... a bona little lattie [a lovely little flat] stocked with gin. Faster driver.

B   Take it easy will ya, we don't want any trouble with Betty Bracelet [the Police].

A   Keep your riah [hair] on, we're immune [safe]. We're girls in uniform ... Wrens on shore-leave starring Diana Durbin and Gracie Fields.

B   Shut your mouth.

A   I should be in Hollywood ... Carmen Miranda eat your hat out.

The conductor arrives, they pay their fare, and he leaves.

A   Do you think she's on the team [do you think he (the conductor) is Gay]?

B   Who?

A	The ommie [man] in the bijou capella [pretty hat].
B	You don't fancy him do ya?
A	I don't know. Bona brandy [Lovely ???]... bona drag [lovely clothes] too.
B	Shut your screech [mouth], he's coming back.

Gay men used Polari much earlier than this. Referred to elsewhere variously as Parlyaree, Parliaree, Parlarie, and Parlare, this name, like much of its lexicon originates from Italian, *parlare* meaning to speak. The variety of spelling reflects the spoken nature of Gayspeak. Language research has traditionally focused on the written form highly regarded by the dominant culture; spoken language, until recently perceived as incorrect and of low status, has consequently been neglected. Sociolinguistic research has had an anthropological and gender bias (Coates 1993, pp 38-57) (2). We believe that Gayspeak, spoken language outside traditional research concerns, the argot of a marginalised group, has been triply neglected.

When Polari was discussed in print, until quite recently, the fact that its users were Gay was hidden: the TV Times (Gordeno 1969, p 40) glossed Polari as the 'dancer's language' thus requiring skilled reading between the lines to make the Gay association; and Partridge (1948b, p 117) linked Polari only to "showmen and strolling players". However, the title of his article, Parlyaree, Cinderella among languages, can be construed as a Gay reference: Polari, overtly viewed as a beautiful creature occasionally brought into the limelight, is associated with the name of a pantomime heroine, suggestive of the core pantomime elements of crossdressing, the related sexual ambiguity, and also the outrageous or camp[3] wordplay and verbal duelling. The process of framing Gay culture in camp theatrical terms is a form of **minstrellisation** (McIntosh 1973, p 8) that renders it acceptable to the dominant culture. Entertainers such as Kenneth Williams, Frankie Howard, and Larry Grayson have popularised Gay culture but only within limits established by the dominant culture. The entertainer Julian Clary has recently challenged this practice. To a camp performance which would be acceptable to the dominant culture, he has added a personal outing making his Gay sexuality a necessary backdrop to the total performance: where there was ambiguous innuendo before, there is now an unmistakable public airing of Gay culture.

In the eighteenth century, Polari was used by itinerant actors and showmen. Individual terms appeared in dictionaries by 1823 (Partridge 1948b, p 116). Hancock (1973 and 1984) makes the link between Polari and **Lingua Franca**, the Romance-based pidgin dating from the Crusades containing words from many Mediterranean languages spoken by sailors plying the Mediterranean Sea. The link resulted from the former sailors who found employment as pedlars and strolling players. By the nineteenth century, Polari was largely centred on theatrical circles. Perhaps we should read Gay circles for theatrical circles, but it is possible that Gay actors carried Polari from wider theatre use into Gay culture. By the mid-twentieth century, Polari was viewed as Gay slang by many Gay men. Early writers made no link between Polari and Gayspeak, and then did so tentatively: Hancock referring to Gordeno (1969) states that

> ... it is also a fact that almost all of the terms listed in the article are known to, and used freely by, the male homosexual subculture - in London at least - which overlaps into the theatrical world. (Hancock, 1973, p 35)

A more confident link was then made:

> ... the connection with male (and not, apparently, female) homosexual speech is also through the sea and the theatre, milieux which have traditionally been comfortable ones for homosexuals. (Hancock 1984, p 394-5)

Lingua Franca may connect more directly with Gayspeak via the port association of sailors and Gay men. This may explain the relative strength of Polari in port cities such as Liverpool, Bristol, Manchester, and London where marginalised cultures have tended to flourish. Hancock (1984, p 395), quoting Chesney (1972), suggests that the link between sailors and homosexuality resulted from the "most genuinely professional male prostitution" taking place in "the great ports". Although influenced by army slang, there does seem to be a connection between 'sailor-speak' and the language used by other groups within the more pluralistic society of ports; an indication of this is the more widespread use in cities like Liverpool of Arabic words such as *bint* and *shufti*.

Certain sociological themes emerge from this history. First, Polari was associated with sailors, and the theatre, both historically safe occupations for Gay men. Interviewees for Channel 4 (1993) make a distinction between London East End Polari, elaborate and influenced by the docks and maritime associations, and West End Polari, 'standard' and influenced by theatrical associations. Second, Polari has been associated with marginalised groups such as tinkers, pedlars, criminals, and prostitutes, all classifiable as "underworld groups" (Burton 1979, p 23). Gay men, also marginalised, have been viewed with similar disdain. Third, just as some marginalised groups developed secret codes, such as criminals' **Cant**[4] or tinkers' **Shelta**[5] (Hancock 1984), so Gay men developed Polari. These codes[6] developed from the need to express common identity, for self-protection, and for secrecy. Fourth, Polari functioned as a street language, operating in a similar way to other urban 'lingos' like backslang - *yob* from boy, and rhyming slang -

apple and pears for stairs. Not surprisingly, some items are present in both Polari and Cockney such as *bevvy, scarper, naff*, and *carsey*. They have become more widely known as both Cockney and camp acting have enjoyed a higher status in the wider community. The word *camp* is itself a Polari word.

Camp acting reached a popular high with the characters of Jules and Sandy played by Hugh Paddick and Kenneth Williams in Round the Horne (BBC 1988), a radio programme from the 1960's. These sketches, representative of 'stage' Polari, contain older items and modern coinage in a playful vein. Simmonds (1988) claims that this language was invented for the series by the script writers Barry Took and Marty Feldman. Here, Kenneth Horne is interviewing Jules and Sandy, directors of an innovative film company called Bona Prods:

S   You see we've got a small independent unit ... film unit.

J   Small budget pictures really.

KH   Would I have varda-ed [seen] any of them do you think?

S   Oh, he's got all the Polari i'n' he.

J   I wonder where he picks it up?

S   Mm..Mm..Yes... well Mr Horne you may have varda-ed one of our tiny bijou [pretty] masterpiece - ettes heartface ... one of our pictures we made was, 'Funny Eke [face]' and 'My Fair Palone [lady].'

KH   I take it you're engaged in something pretty exciting at the moment?

J   Yes, we're going to do Samson and Delilah.

S   C'mon Jul'. How do you see it, how do you see it?

J   Well I see ... I see Samson all huge and all butch [masculine].

S   Butch, yes, yes.

J   Great bulging thews and wopping great lallies [legs].

S   Yes, yes, yes.

J   The film opens with him lying there spark out on his palliase.

S   Oh.

J   And suddenly there's a movement behind the arras.

S   Yes, yes.

J   And who comes trolling [wandering] in, but this palone [woman] Delilah ... she vardas [sees] his sleeping eke [face] and she pulls out this pair of scissors and lops off his riah [hair].

S   Yes I can see that ... yes great close up of his head, nanti riah [without any hair].

J   Yes, then the Philistines come and they mock him, Mr Horne.

S   Oh they mock him ... what a figure of tragedy he represents.

J   Then they drag him up to the king's lattie [place] and chain him.

S   Oooh.

J   And chain him by his lallies [legs] to the pillar.

S   Oooh oooh!

J   Then he gets his wild up.

S   Wild up, yes, yes.

J   And with one mighty heave-hoh he brings the whole lattie [place] tumbling about their heads ... end of film.

S   Bravo Jul'. Bravo, its an Oscar winnner.

This further example incorporates the Polari items which seem to be most widely known:

As feely homies [young men], when we launched ourselves on the gay scene, Polari was all the rage. We would zhoosh [fix] our riahs [hair], powder our eeks [faces], climb into our bona [nice] new drag [clothes], don our batts [shoes] and troll off [cruise] to some bona bijou [nice, small] bar. In the bar, we would stand around parlyaring [chatting] with our sisters [gay acquaintances], varda [look at] the bona [nice] cartes [genitals] on the butch [male] homie [man] ajax [nearby] who, if we fluttered our ogleriahs [eyelashes], might just troll over [wander over] to offer a light. (Burton 1979, p 23)

Burton (1979) lists about 50 Polari items and Hancock (1984) more than 100. Just how many of these terms were in wide use is not clear, but many users give the same example when interviewed - *varda the bona ommie* meaning look at the beautiful man - suggesting widespread currency of only a few clichéd items.

There is some evidence, although Hancock (1984, p 394) raises some doubts about this, that London Lesbians in the 1940/50's used a modified version of Polari. This is an area requiring further study (Hayes 1976, p 266). The following dialogue (Channel 4, 1993) is between two Lesbians returning home after a night out:

A   Did you see that butch number [masculine Lesbian] with the big martini [pinkie ring?] on her? She said I had the look of a Lena Horne.

B   Honestly, one compliment from a palone [woman] going as Cliff Richard and you go all femmie [feminine].

A   She did not look like Cliff Richard. She was much butcher [more masculine].

B   I thought she was married to that piece in the cashmere and crimplene.

A   What George? You must be joking. He makes Liberace look like a lumberjack.

B   Anyhow, she was so busy smooching with that one in the lucoddy [body] suit that I didn't get a look in.

A   No, neither did I tonight. Mind you, some nights I like just looking.

B   Mmm.

A   All those lovely lallies [legs].

B   Tall ones, short ones, some as big as ya hat.

This historical picture reveals how Polari was adopted and developed playfully by the Gay community for reasons of self-protection, secrecy, and statement of common identity. With decriminalisation in 1967, and the emergence of an increasingly confident open Gay culture, the first and second reasons lost much of their strength. Changing political values also cast an unfavourable light on Polari as this dialogue (Channel 4, 1993) illustrates:

D   Honestly Tony you are so self-oppressed. All this camp, bitchy chat is so sexist like. It really puts down women and Gay men.

Tony   Its called Polari. Words like *camp* and *gay*, *fab* and *groovy* - they've entered the language.

D   Just listen to yourself. 'Entered' - that is a revolting metaphor. You are a slave to phallocentric discourse without even realising it.

Tony   Oh that's just the madcap fun-loving Stalinist in you ducky.

There was also criticism of Polari's outmoded inter-sex view of Gay sexuality, a view illustrated by the actual term for a Gay man - *ommie-palone*, literally meaning man-woman. For many writers, Polari was flawed politically:

... although gay slang is the vocabulary of people who are them-selves outcasts from the straight culture, it is also sexist, classist, and racist, and the existence of terms that reflect such attitudes binds us to the same value system that makes us outcasts. Such a conflict within the gay subculture will not be resolved easily and there are two possible solutions that gay militants have chosen as strategies for eradicating such values from the liberation movement. (Stanley 1974, p 386)

The first of the solutions she mentions is the avoidance of all Gayspeak, not so as to hide Gay identity

... but rather to stop the process of alienation and ghettoisation and to reject the value system which Gayspeak has incorporated from the mainstream culture. (Hayes 1976, p 262)

The second is the process of value redefinition adopted by Black and Feminist movements where terms are repossessed and reloaded in connotation by the marginalised groups in question. This process is a conscious attempt by radical Gays to manipulate the relationship between langauge and behaviour (Hayes 1976, p 261). Two decades ago, McIntosh (1973, p 9) asked whether we should embrace the word 'queer' in the same way that 'black' had been embraced by Blacks in the United States. Clearly, that has now happened, but some Polari survives. The linguistic-political debate hasn't brought about a streamlined unified picture of language use in Gay culture. McIntosh assesses the impact of the debate as follows:

... the emergence of liberation movements has proved that gay people can escape this ambivalence [society's minstrellising tolerance of certain aspects of Gay culture and rejection of most others], an escape which involves a struggle against the straight values we have all internalised from an early age. The gay ghetto turns these aside with a joke; the new movements dig them out and defuse them. Interestingly enough, in doing so they become very self-conscious about language, aware that if the way people see the world is to be reformed then language, the means by which we share our understanding, must be reformed too. In some groups there is a reluctance to abstain altogether from parlare; it represents, after all, whatever warmth and solidarity the gay world was able to create. (McIntosh, 1973, p 9)

Philosophies conflict here: on the one hand, language reform is a prerequisite for social change - if Gayspeak reproduces the undesirable attitudes of the dominant culture then Gay culture becomes defined in some ways by the same attitudes, thus necessitating major re-evaluation; on the other, language is part and parcel of identity - if Gayspeak is as much a product of Gay identity and culture as it is of the dominant culture, then to deny it any validity or function, is a denial of some aspects of Gay culture. The radical perspective denigrates Gayspeak references to sex roles and sexuality couched in dominant culture values. If these references are seen as parodic or comic, then Gayspeak confirms Gay identity by comically undermining those dominant values (Hayes 1976, p 264).

We believe that both positions bear upon the marginalisation of Gay culture: the first reflecting the negative element in that marginalisation, the second the positive elements in Gay culture including the warmth and solidarity McIntosh refers to. Whilst not denying the first position, we describe the more positive features of current Gayspeak below.

Gayspeak - Current Vitality

To establish the productive and receptive knowledge of Gayspeak, both in and outside the Gay community, we undertook a survey based on a questionnaire (Appendix A). The first section focused on the personal background of the informant; age, gender, sexuality, level of urbanisation, and proximity to Gay culture. The second attempts to assess the level of overt knowledge of

1) older items
2) cross-over items between Gay culture and mainstream culture
3) newer items.

Informants were given little context and no actual terms to prompt their responses. The third section was designed to assess the receptive knowledge of items in the same categories and the last section sought to enlarge our knowledge of current Gayspeak. A range of people from different subgroups within Britain were questioned. From this survey, these initial conclusions were drawn:

1) Older items are productively used mainly by Gay men over thirty-five in cities who came out relatively early in life. Stock phrases are slightly more widely known.
2) Cross-over items are receptively known by a wide range of younger city dwellers. However, some items eg *naff* undergo a complete change of meaning as they pass from Gay use to wider use. For younger interviewees, there are often current items more readily available than the ones in our survey.

112

3) Newer items are widely known by younger people belonging to the scene or who have frequent contact with members from it.

There seems to be a correlation between the amount of Gayspeak used by Gay men and their level of involvement on the Gay scene. Lesbians do not score especially highly in any area, perhaps confirming the existence of a separate female Gay argot or indeed the absence of one.

We recognise that this survey was limited in various ways and that much more detailed work remains to be done in this area. By focusing solely on vocabulary items, the survey was limited in scope; by interviewing tens rather than hundreds, it was limited in extent; and by using an uncontextualised test-like research instrument, it lacked validity in that Gayspeak is used informally in specifically definable contexts. Many Gay interviewees use a range of Gayspeak items within appropriate contexts, but they found it difficult to shift register and produce Gayspeak in the inappropriate context of the questionnaire. The difficulties inherent in conducting research interviews with Gay men has been described by Leznoff (1956).

Whereas our survey was concerned with British Gayspeak, the most extensive Gayspeak lexicon (Rogers 1972) gives over 12,000 mainly American entries. Farrell (1972), also concerned with American Gayspeak, lists 233 items. This US bias in lexical data mirrors the higher level of Gay politicization in the USA. Our description of early Gayspeak concerned British usage but the American researchers throw out many ideas for assessing current Gayspeak. For Farrell (1972, p 3), the major function of Gayspeak is the ordering and classifying of experience, interests, and problems, within Gay culture. Similarly, Hayes (1972, p 258) identifies the habit of categorization according to the Gay parameters of:

1) separation of outsiders from insiders
2) accounting for ambiguous persons within social-sexual interactions
3) description of the relationships of insiders.

Farrell (1972, p 3) notes the predominance of Gayspeak items relating to social types of homosexual, ways of making sexual contacts, and varieties of sexual acts. Hayes (1972, p 259) categorizes major Gayspeak lexical areas into:

1) physical appearance ie height, weight
2) sexual preference eg *bottom boy*
3) intimacy of relationships eg *sister, auntie, mother*

113

4) rank within the subculture eg *queen bee*
5) eccentricities within the norms of the subculture eg *leather queen.*

A frequency order of Farrell's list is revealing. He has references to:

1) the categorization of people according to their sexual behaviour or preference, eg *green queens* - Gay men who enjoy sex in public parks, *steam bath bennie* - Gay men who frequent public steam baths (88 items)
2) sexual acts, eg a *circle jerk* - masturbating simultaneously in a circle, a *Mazola party* - group sex when the participants are covered in corn oil (53)
3) body parts, eg *schlong, bird, dong, noony* - all meaning penis (20 items)
4) social activities such as cruising, going out, and gossiping, eg *read* - to argue or otherwise engage in witty conversation (11 items)
5) people's behaviour, eg *carry on like a white woman* - to behave in a girlish way (9 items)
6 a)the Police, eg *Alice, Fuzz, Lilly Law* (8 items)
   b)appearance, eg *super star* - a narcissistic Gay (8 items)
   c)places on the scene, eg *gay stream* - the public baths, *a fruit stand* - a Gay bar (8 items)
7) family, hierarchies, and close attachments, eg *mother, daughter* (5 items)

The number quoted in brackets is the approximate number of relevant items in Farrell's lexicon. Little solid documentation exists on the differences between American and British Gayspeak but just as mainstream culture has enjoyed jokes based upon the *braces/suspenders* ambiguity so have the two Gay cultures. Armistead Maupin, the American author of the Tales of the City series, makes use of these differences. After reading a copy of Gay News, the character Mouse muses:

> ... judging from the classified ads, Gay Englishmen were perpetually searching for attractive 'uncles' (daddies) with 'stashes' (mustaches), who were 'non-scene' (never in bars) and 'non-camp' (butch). (Maupin, A., 1990, p 124)

Clearly, the cultural differences between the USA and Britain are mirrored by linguistic differences, no more so than in Gay culture. Because of the open upfront attitudes of North Americans in comparison to the reticence of the British, the verbalization of activities common to both societies occurs more in the USA than in Britain: Gay men cruise parks in both countries, but only American Gayspeak has a term, *green queen*, to describe them. Similarly, the open public face of Gay culture in cities such as San Francisco and New York, resulting for example in the bathhouse scene, has produced US-only terminology to describe that scene, eg *a bathsheba, our lady of the vapours*. We note that social categorization eg *Safeway queen* and fashion reference have a higher frequency in Britain than in the USA; and sexual categorization and body references seem less frequent in Britain. However, the Gay scene in Britain becomes increasingly Americanized as the common use of *buns, cruise*, and *pecs* illustrates.

Observation and participation in Gay interaction suggests that certain themes recur in Britain. These include the general areas of

1)   the performing arts
2)   the visual arts
3)   the decorative arts.

Underlying all of these is a sense of camp (Sontag 1964). More specifically under the performing arts, these themes centre on female film stars who combined elements of tragedy, glamour, and power in their film roles and sometimes in their private lives. These stars have been described as exaggerations of female stereotyped roles (Hayes 1976, p 260). A Gay pantheon would include: Bette Davis, Judy Garland, Marilyn Monroe, Barbara Stanwick, Marlene Dietrich, Mae West, and Barbara Streisand. Other Gay sensibilities here centre on Busby Berkely choreography, ballet, musicals, and theatrical references generally. Under visual arts, we find references to fashion and references to photography, particularly to Ritts, Weber, Mablethorpe, Hartnell, and Man Ray; allusions to fine arts include the Pre-Raphaelite School and David Hockney. Under decorative arts, types of interior design based on Art Deco, Art Nouveau, and Osborne & Little soft furnishings predominate, as do references to antiques, and the house and garden.

It has already been mentioned that Gay men enjoy persiflage: *dishing* and *reading* are Gayspeak labels for this. *Camp*, "at its very core ... the art of the put-down" (Hayes 1974 p 260) is the ultimate persiflage. The playful wordsmithery found in general English such as *hoity toity, arty farty*, and *mish mash* has more than an echo in Gayspeak's *trolley dolly, chubby chaser*, and *fag hag*. The productiveness of general English has been well documented (eg Collins Cobuild 1990 p 113) eg the pattern in English, *sloppy-ish, vague-ish*, and *Blue Peter-ish* where 'ish' means in the manner of, or of similar quality to, which can be extended ad infinitum. Gayspeak is also very productive: *drama queen, drag queen, size queen*, and *ruched curtain queen.* Hayes (1974 p 259) notes that this compounding productiveness is a rich seam in current Gayspeak used to classify the subgroups within Gay culture. An extension of this is the comic trivialisation of expected expressions. Examples of this can be seen in the 1940's Polari dialogue quoted above: "Carmen Miranda eat your hat out"; "a mere powder compact's throw from here" (Channel 4 1993). The second example also contains an element of feminising of the kind discussed below. For Hayes (1974 p 260), this trivialisation displays a cynicism which turns it into a kind of mimicry parodying dominant culture and mocking mainstream sexual stereotypes.

As with all 'non-standard' usage, Gayspeak's current parameters change from city to city, day to day, and person to person. Although our analysis may not tally with individual experience, we believe that the linguistic vitality we describe reflects the high status awarded to verbal performance in Gay culture.

The Feminising Aspect

So far we have seen the frequency with which 'feminine' references occur in both Polari and more current Gayspeak: *ommie-palone* for Gay man, *'ambag* for money, *powder compact's throw* for stone's throw, the use of female role models as reference points, and feminine pronouns and words for female family relations eg *sister*. Gay radicals, Lesbians, and feminists have all taken issue with the Gay adoption of 'feminine' aspects that are caricatures of women, and therefore contributory to the sexism latent in society. Objections could also be voiced about the adoption of 'masculine' aspects that caricature men eg leather equating to butch, militarism to manliness. This criticism seems to maintain the dominant viewpoint that the 'feminine' is universally negatively-loaded, whereas the 'masculine' is positively-loaded: tomboys are accepted, sissies not. Radical movements attack Gayspeak for ignoring the load attached to roles. But it could be argued that the adoption of a feminising aspect in Gay culture is an example of role-reclaiming matching label-reclaiming; by ignoring the fact that men should play only 'masculine' roles, it questions the accepted division of roles along gender lines.

A recently observed situation illustrates the subtleties of such gender-blending. A Gay couple and a straight couple were socialising together as is their custom. In their interaction, the Gay men continued to use feminine pronouns such as *she*, and *her* for each other, the woman, and also, on occasion, for the straight man. The woman found it easy to reciprocate the usage but the straight man could not. In this way Gay culture stretches out to embrace sympathetic outsiders. McIntosh (1973 p 9) describes how Gay men use pronouns both to identify fellow Gays in a non-Gay situation eg "Do you think she's on the team?" (Channel 4 1993) and for any male displaying sensibilities acceptable to Gay culture. The 'feminising' usage of the woman is non-loaded because she does not carry the dominant cultural load. The straight man's reticence derives from the automatic denigratory load carried when straight men use 'feminising' language. This points to the potential of the Gay situation for countering sexism in society by making gender division subservient to Attitude. In this light, the Polari term *ommie-palone*, instead of being ditched as unsound, could be used with pride if the 'maleness' and 'femaleness' in all men is recognised. Straight 'New Age' men have attempted to adopt attributes previously allowable only in women, and so made the same point.

Functions of Language in Gay Culture

We have discussed the functions of Gayspeak within the Gay community but these functions can be seen in a broader sociolinguistic framework. Tajfel (1974, 1978, and 1981) proposes a theory of inter-group relations and social change based on groups whose members have a poor self image and where the group has inferior social status. These members can either reject or accept their social 'inferiority'. If they accept, two courses are open to them: either they measure themselves against members of their own group or they try and join the 'superior' group. The predominance of classifying terms in Gayspeak and the status awarded to *dishing*, could be seen as results of the first of these courses. The second can be instanced by the way in which some public figures deny their Gay sexual orientation and so become targets for outing. Rejection of the label 'inferior' prompts three courses of action immediately recognisable in Gay radicalism: the attempt to assimilate with the 'superior' group and demand equality; the redefinition of negative characteristics; and the creation of new dimensions of comparison.

Hayes (1976) provides a detailed analysis of the sociolinguistic nature of Gayspeak. He identifies three distinct areas: the **secret setting** where Gay orientation is hidden outside the exclusive company of close friends; the **social setting** where Gay men have traditionally been most public; and the **radical-activist setting** where the socio-political nature of all behaviour is acknowledged. These settings are not necessarily person-specific in that people function in changing situations with overlapping settings. As a consequence, Gay men often move from a register containing Gayspeak to one which is more circumspect. This kind of register move is similar, although for different reasons, to the one apparent when people move from one social situation to another eg the infamous telephone voice.

The courses outlined by Tajfel correspond to Hayes' delineation of Gayspeak settings. The intergroup comparison that Tajfel suggests can result from 'inferiority' acceptance matches "the process of categorisation" (1974 p 259) in Hayes' social setting. Tajfel's second course, the move to the superior group, corresponds to the secret setting where Gay men are "painfully self-conscious about the stigma imposed upon them ... and take great pains to avoid any mannerisms or language which would stereotype them" (1974 p 257). The three courses resulting from rejection of 'inferiority' correspond to the radical-activist setting where all behaviour, including language use, is uncompromisingly 'out'.

In our assessment of Polari, the functions of self-protection, secrecy, and statement of common identity were brought out. The need for secrecy has now become a matter of personal conviction rather than legal sanction but the bonding element still remains, a function of the social setting whose vitality and resultant conscious-raising dynamism have been described. The more recent radical perspective has tended to minimise the value of the social function, the "warmth and solidarity" (McIntosh 1973, p 9) generated by Gayspeak. The widespread criticism of secretive, closet Gay culture and the importance attached to an uncompromising radical approach to Gay liberation have both contributed to a lack of recognition of the full validity of the linguistic space afforded by Gayspeak.

One reason for the vitality and dynamism of the finely-crafted performances and one-off throwaways of Gayspeak is the heightened awareness of register that Gay men have as a consequence of their appreciation of social settings. Only in the halls of ideology does all social interaction conform to one political perspective; in the real world, we change register continually to meet the changing sensibilities of different settings - we stop swearing in front of parents and children; we revert to local accents when we return to our roots; we temper our lapsed Catholicism in front of our pious elderly aunts; we couch our jealousies in veiled references in public, saving our vitriol for home; we keep comments for, and from, our partners: in sum, we change what we say and how we say it according to our perception of the overall nuances of a situation.

That such register shifts smack of hypocrisy and enfeebling commitment to The Cause reveals a linguistic naivety and a denial of the value of separate Gay space. It could be argued that continuous use of Gayspeak equates to maximum linguistic freedom. This ignores the frisson that would ensue from the conflict between the default dominant linguistic setting and Gayspeak. It could also serve to undermine the efficacy of Gayspeak as a necessary counterbalance to the dominant settings. Many Gay men have become adept at the register shifts that result from their increased awareness of language-in-context, an awareness that allows them to revel in language's full Gayspeak resonance when the stage is unequivocally theirs.

Conclusions

This article is an unwieldy hybrid of linguistics, politics, sociology, and history, but from it, we hope that the positive, as well as the less attractive, features of Gay language use have been set out, ready for further research. Increased Americanization and further cross-over into dominant culture resulting from 'out' performances will probably be features of future usage. In the increasingly pluralistic, overlapping, segmenting, and pillarized society of cities, the need for linguistic space will no doubt remain paramount. Equally, the habit of register shifts born of a fine perception of situation-specific sensibilities will prove to be an invaluable tool in the evermore complex nature of urban society both at its core and on the margins.

Endnotes

1. The need for linguistic space for marginalised groups in society can be illustrated by the process of **recreolization** noted in cities like Manchester, where the children of Caribbean parents speak more Creole than their parents. This results, we believe, from a desire to express their sense of, and need for, group identity in a society otherwise oblivious to value of that culture.

2. In response to the total-speech-community approach of much linguistic study, Gumperz (1962) argued the case for defining linguistic groups more discretely to match anthropologically-delineated groups. Lakoff (1973 p 45), taking women as such a group, argued that

    > 'women's language' has as foundation the attitude that women are marginal to the serious concerns of life, which are pre-empted by men. The marginality and powerlessness of women is reflected in both the ways women are expected to speak, and the ways in which women are spoken of.

    Tannen pursued the differences between male and female discourse in both an academic (1990a and 1990b) and popularistic vein (1991). Coates (1993) explored similar concerns at considerable length and examined their implications in our society where gender is such a highly significant category.

3. The Random House Dictionary of English Language defines the adjective *camp* as "an ironic or amusing quality present in extravagant gesture, style, or form, especially when inappropriate or out of proportion to the content that is expressed". The slang meaning of the verb is "to speak or act so theatrically or affectedly as to parody one's own personality, characteristics, or role in life". Brien (1967, pp 873-4) defines *camp* as "speaking almost entirely in italics, of tarting up ideas with costume jewellery, of insulating emotions by ironically exaggerating them". He lists the works of the artists Mozart, El Greco, Rimbaud, Dostoevsky, Firbank, and Coward as camp, and regards all aspects of Oscar Wilde as the ultimate in camp. Susan Sontag (1964) provides a deeper analysis of 'campness' and offers a longer, complimentary canon. She describes the "peculiar affinity" between camp taste and Gay culture, noting that "homosexuals, by and large, constitute the vanguard - and the most articulate audience - of camp",

one reason being the obvious suitability of camp's metaphor of life as theatre for a "certain aspect of the situation of homosexuals" (Sontag 1964, p 529).

4. Some writers make this link overt: Rogers' (1972, Introduction) aim was "to make available a dictionary of homophile cant".

5. A form of Shelta or Tinker Talk is still alive in the slang usage of Irish travelling children living in Manchester.

6. Sykes (1958, pp 85-6) argues that a marginalised group such as prisoners provides itself with a sort of shorthand which compresses the variegated range of its experience into a manageable framework. By distinguishing and naming we prepare ourselves for action ... the activities of group members are no longer an undifferentiated stream of events; rather, they have been analyzed, classified, given labels; and these labels supply an evaluation and interpretation of experience as well as a set of convenient names. Words ... carry a penumbra of admiration and disapproval, of attitude and belief, which channels and controls the behaviour of the individual who uses them or to whom they are applied.

Appendix A

To assess both the productive and receptive knowledge of Polari words and more recent Gayspeak vocabulary items, we used a questionnaire as the basis for interviews. In these interviews, the items mentioned or the concerns raised in the questionnaire acted as prompts for more wide-ranging discussion. We purposefully interviewed as wide a range of people as possible as we wanted to assess the extent of Gayspeak knowledge in the wider urban community as well as in differing Gay subgroups. We attempted to classify interviewees according to the parameters of

1) Age: Which age range do you belong to?

    a) 0-20   b) 21-25   c) 26-30   d) 31-35
    e) 36-40   f) 41-45   g) 46-50   h) 51-60
    i) 60+

2) Gender: Which sex label best describes you?

    a) female   b) male   c) transsexual   d) other

3) Orientation: Which sexual orientation label best describes you?

    a) gay   b) lesbian   c) bisexual   d) heterosexual
    e) other

4) Class: Which class label best describes you?

    a) working class   b) lower middle class
    c) middle class   d) upper middle class
    e) upper class   f) other

5) Urbanization: i) In what kind of environment were you brought up?

    a) rural   b) small town   c) suburbs
    d) inner city   e) metropolis   f) other

ii) To what degree are you urbanized nowadays?

a) not at all   b) a little
c) quite a lot   d) completely

6)   Familiarity: Tick the statement below that best describes
      you.

Do not know or socialize with gay people
Know some gay people but do not tend to socialize with
them
Socialize with gay people but not usually on the gay
scene
Socialize with gay people quite often on the gay scene
Socialize mainly with gay people on the scene

7)   Language awareness: How interested in language(s) are
      you?

a) not at all   b) a little
c) quite a lot   d) very

We also wanted to assess how widely used and how well known Gayspeak
is. From earlier Polari word lists and our own experience, we chose ten items
of older Gayspeak (Polari), ten items which we felt had crossed over into the
wider community sometimes with a change in meaning, and ten newer items.
Initially, we only gave interviewees a prompt or gloss (eg. You want to say
that something/someone is very good) and asked them if they knew and/or
used a Gayspeak item for the prompted situation (eg. 'bona'). We then
showed the interviewees the thirty items and asked them if they recognised,
used, and/or could define these words. As a result of the interviews, we
compiled our own wordlist divided into the same three categories. Here is
an extract from our list.

Survey Questionnaire

Older Gayspeak	Cross-Over Items	Newer Items
Affair(e)	AC/DC	Bitch
Bats	Bevvy	Buns
Bijou	Bimbo	Butch
Bona	Camp	Chicken
Charver	Carsey	Cruise
Eke	Cottage	Dabble
Frock	Drag	Dish
Karts	Dyke	Fag hag
Lallies	Faggot	Nellie
Latty	Mankey	Queen
Nanti	Naff	Rent boy
Ogle	Palaver	Rim
Ogleriahs	Ponce	Rough trade
Ommie	Punk	Swish
Ommie-palone	Scarper	Trade
Palone		Trolley-dolly
Polari		Dinge queen
Savvy		Disco queen
Slap		Drama queen
Troll		Leather queen
Varda		Rent queen
Voche		Rice queen
Vogues		Size queen
Walloper		

Bibliography

Ardener, S., (ed), (1975) *Perceiving Women*, Mallaby Press, London.

Ardener, S. (1978a) "The Nature of Women in Society" in Ardener, S. (ed) *Perceiving Women*, Mallaby Press, London.

Ardener, S. (1978b) *Defining Females* Croom Helm, London.

BBC (1988) *Round the Horn* (audio cassette).

Brien, A. (1967) "Camper's Guide", *The New Statesman* 23, pp 373-4.

Burton, P. (1979) "The Gentle Art of Confounding Naffs", in *Gay News* 120, p 23.

Carol, A. & Warren, B. (1974) *Identity and Community in the Gay World*, John Wiley, New York.

Channel 4 (1993) "A Storm in a Tea-Cup" in *Summer's Out* 19/08/93.

Chesney, K. (1972) *The Victorian Underworld*, Schocken, New York.

Coates, J. (1993) *Men, Women, and Society*, Longman, London.

Collins Cobuild (1990) *English Grammar*, Harper Collins, London.

Dorval, B. (ed) (1990) *Conversational Organisation and its Development*, Ablex, Norwood, NJ.

Farrell, R. A. (1972) "The Argot of the Homosexual Subculture", *Anthropological Linguistics* 14, pp 97-109.

Gordeno, P. (1969) "The Walloper's Polari", *The TV Times* October 16, p 40.

Gumperz, J. J. (1962) "Types of Linguistic Communities", *Anthropological Linguistics* 4/1, pp 28-40.

Hancock, I. (1973) "Remnants of Lingua Franca in Britain", *The University of South Florida Language Quarterly* 12, pp 35-6.

Hancock, I. (1984) "Shelta and Polari", Trudgill, P. (1984) *The Languages of the British Isles*, CUP, Cambridge.

Hancock, I. (1984) "Shelta and Polari", Trudgill, P. (1984) *The Languages of the British Isles*, CUP, Cambridge.

Hayes, J. J. (1976) "Gayspeak", *The Quarterly Journal of Speech* 62, pp 256-266.

Hotten, J. (1864) *The Slang Dictionary* London.

Humphreys, L. (1972) *Out of the Closet ; the Sociology of Homosexual Liberation*, Prentice Hall, Englewood Cliffs NJ.

Lakoff, R. (1973) "Language and Women's Place", *Language in Society* 2, p 75.

Leznoff, M. (1956) "Interviewing Homosexuals", *The American Journal of Sociology* LXII (July) pp 202-4.

Maupin, A. (1990) *Babycakes*, Black Swan, London.

McIntosh, M. (1973) "Gayspeak", *Lunch* 16, pp 7-9.

Partridge, E. (1948) *Here, There, and Everywhere. Essays Upon Language*, Hamish Hamilton, London.

Partridge, E. (1970) *Slang Today and Yesterday*, Routledge Kegan Paul, London.

Rogers, B. (1972) *The Queen's Vernacular*, Straight Arrow Books, San Francisco.

Simmonds, J. (1975) Sleeve Notes, *BBC (1988)*

Sontag, S (1964) "Notes on Camp", *The Partisan Review* 31, pp 515-30.

Stanley, J. P. (1970) "Homosexual Slang", *American Speech* 45, pp 45-59.

Stanley, J. P. (1974) "When we say 'Out of the Closets!'", *College English* 36, pp 385-91.

Tajfel, H. (1974) "Social identity and intergroup behaviour", *Social Science Information*, 13 (2), pp 65-93.

Sykes, G. (1958) *The Society of Captives,* Princeton University Press, Princeton NJ.

Tajfel, H. (ed) (1978) *Differentiation Between Social Groups: Studies in the Social Psychology of Intergroup Relations*, Academic Press, London.

Tajfel, H. (1981) *Human Groups and Social Categories*, CUP, Cambridge.

Tannen, D. (1990a) "Gender differences in conversational coherence: physical alignment and topical cohesion" in Dorval, B. (ed) (1990) *Conversational Organisation and its Development*, Ablex, Norwood NJ.

Tannen, D. (1990b) "Gender differences in topical cohesion: creating involvement in best friends' talk", *Discourse Processes*, 13 (1) pp, 73-90.

Tannen, D. (1991) *You Just Don't Understand: Women and Men in Conversation*, Virago, London.

Trudgill, P. (1984) *The Languages of the British Isles*, CUP, Cambridge.

7 Bi-sexuality – A place on the margins

David Bell

Is the bisexual not merely marginal to conventional sexual categories but, as some commentators aver, as a social and cultural being non-existent? (Evans, 1993, p 148)

This book has an interesting title: *The Margins of the City*. I wasn't sure when I first heard it whether its tone was celebratory or commiseratory. And the margins certainly exist in a similarly ambiguous position in a lot of current theorizing around issues such as 'race' (especially perhaps in 'post-colonial' and 'multicultural' discourses), gender and sexuality. There's lots of talk of 'border critics', about how being 'out there' is a good vantage point from which to interrogate what's 'in there'(or is it 'in here'?), wherever the 'in', the 'centre', might be (and most people are rapidly trying to get away from it, to break out to their own margin). Writers like feminist critic bell hooks (sic) see the margin as the space for the "formation of counter-hegemonic cultural practice", describing it as a "space of radical openness - a profound edge" and as "the site of radical possibility, a space of resistance" (hooks, 1991, p 145, 149). And Sidonie Smith (1987, p 176) writes that "while margins have their limitations they also have their advantages of vision. They are polyvocal, more distant from the centers of power and conventions of selfhood. They are heretical". We get to hear a lot more about 'advantages of vision' than 'limitations'. But the margin is also a treacherous and slippery place to be in. It can be a site of resistance, certainly, but it can also be an exclusion zone, a cordoned-off little corner where the marginalised are free to play out their rage and their strategies of opposition at a safe distance from the horses and anything or anyone else they might frighten. As Linda McDowell (1992, p 65) says, "there is little reason to celebrate a marginality that entails lack of power". In addition, voices from these marginal spaces are so often recuperated by patronising and oppressive forces, who celebrate our authentic otherness and exoticness, pat us on the head, and drag us out to parade their liberal and enlightened attitudes (Jackson, 1993).

Life On A Margin

So, what about these *margins*? Where are they? Who occupies them? And do they like it there? The particular margins I want to think about in this chapter are those theoretical and political margins into which bisexuality is eagerly thrust by, among others, heterosexist society and the oppositional cultures of lesbian and gay communities. They are very real margins, complete with the contradictions that I've tried to outline above. For some, the place of bisexuality is a terrific vantage point from which to view what goes on in either 'heterosoc' (as Derek Jarman (1992) has termed it) or 'gay life', and to expose its failings, inconsistencies and bigotries. Well, that's all well and good. That's the margin as a site of resistance; political, playful, and with its own kinds of power. But for others, the place of bisexuality is a not-space, a theoretical and actual nonexistent thing; it only exists in the naive minds of those poor souls too timid to come down off their fences and be straight or gay (Eadie, 1992). As David Evans (1993, p 148) says, "there would appear to be no social space for bisexual forms". And for a lot of bisexual people, it's that kind of marginalisation we feel - it's being excluded from 'straight' society and from 'gay spaces', whether they be clubs, political bodies, marches and campaigns, or theories, histories and positions.

And that's why this chapter is called 'Bisexuality - a place on the margins?'. It's meant to be an ironic question; a question which works in a number of different ways. Should bisexuality be on the margins? On whose margins is it, anyway? If it is marginal, is that good or bad? And I want to try and think about what I've elsewhere called the *trouble* with bisexuality (Bell, 1993), which is another multi-layered phrase: by trouble, I mean the trouble that bisexuality causes for those tied to dualistic ways of thinking; I also mean the trouble that being bisexual causes, the trouble it gets us into; and also my own particular troubles with the way bisexuality is written and theorized. Of course, theorizing is never enough. There's also the trouble of trying to make some of these ideas real. Start to think about something which we might call a 'bisexual community' or even a 'bisexual identity' or a 'bisexual politics', and how it might actually work on a day-to-day level for those people who might want to belong to it or subscribe to it or at least be supportive of it, and you really do get into trouble...

The Case of the Disappearing Bisexual

Let's kick off with an anecdote. Picture the scene: the final session of a two-day conference, billed as being concerned with 'lesbian, gay, bisexual politics'. Two distinguished theorists from 'Lesbian and Gay Studies' [sic] have delivered papers which, despite dealing with gender on the one hand

and transgression on the other (and despite having just heard a 'review' of the conference's handling of bisexuality), fail to mention what had become by this time 'the B-word', the unmentionable third of the conference's theme, occasionally slipped in by other speakers, usually in the manner of 'lesbian and gay ... *andbisexualorwhatever*', as a hurried whisper, an unpleasant taste, through gritted teeth; but more often ignored altogether, even in keynote speeches about diversity. During question time, someone (and it wasn't me) asked about this ignoring of bisexuality, and received the following replies: that bisexuality doesn't exist beyond some kind of Freudian notion of infantile polymorphous perversity, some kind of unsocialised, undifferentiated, *basic instinct* which is soon reshaped. Or, that bisexuality may exist as a particular *perversion*, but that it might just as well not exist, since it has no identity (unlike homosexuality, which has the Foucauldian figure of 'the homosexual' to identify it). Suddenly, a number of people in the audience felt ourselves vanishing ... *The Case of the Disappearing Bisexual*, as it were. Or, in Judith Butler's (1991, p 20) words, we were projected into "a domain of unthinkability and unnameability". There it is, the margin. The place off the map. And being there that day didn't feel much like a great position of critical resistance. It felt like being written out.

Stacey Young (1991) has celebrated our trouble-making marginality as part of the 'postmodern dilemma'. And that's all well and good, if you want to live your life as the walking embodiment of postmodernism. But that seems a little rose-tinted to me. I certainly don't want to be just part of the postmodern dilemma (although I think there are times when it's fun to confuse people, to force them to rethink some of their ideas, and maybe persuade them - as that great bisexual button says - to "Assume Nothing"; but sometimes it's just a nuisance, since we're too often called to account for not fitting other people's assumptions). I don't want to always be standing on the margins pointing and laughing as those inside trip over their suppositions. Because at the end of the day that makes us annoying (not that there's anything wrong with being annoying; it's just that sometimes it would be nice to move beyond irritant to a fuller level of participation: I for one am sick of having to keep nudging, coughing, raising eyebrows to remind people to include me in their discussions; it would be far nicer to be there, able to join in, able to help things move on from the rather sorry state they've been stuck in for what seems like eternity). But it's beginning to feel like bisexuality will only ever inhabit that irritating marginality, since it's just too troublesome, for a number of reasons.

The Trouble With Bisexuality

Part of the trouble with bisexuality is obviously that it doesn't fit into our dualistic way of thinking. It isn't homo, and it isn't hetero - it's neither and both, at the same time. Whichever way you look at it, somehow we can't be made to fit; and anyone who doesn't fit existing frames of reference is a troublemaker. As Kathleen Bennett (1992, p 215) says, "Bisexuality has the potential to challenge essentialist hierarchical dualism at its very roots by refusing to accept the necessity to dichotomize". But dichotomies are very useful to people; "dualism", writes Susan Bordo (1992, p 161), "is easier to 'go beyond' in theory than in practice". A dualism like hetero/homo offers security, positionality, identity. We can deconstruct it, rupture it, *in theory*, but to try and *challenge* it, well, that's never going to be a position of strength so long as it's pushing against such strongly-held beliefs. And the hetero/homo dualism is very strongly held. Read any accounts of bisexual coming-out and you'll see what I mean.

And this brings me to one of my own troubles with bisexuality. There seem to me to be two major alternatives to this hetero/homo split currently on offer from within bisexual thinking: the replacement of the dyad with a hetero/bi/homo triad; or the abolition of categories altogether. So many times, people had said "I'm not *bi*sexual, I'm just *sexual*" - or, as was recently discussed in the magazine *Bifrost*, "I'm fully sexual", or "I'm a person with sexuality" (Pink Dandelion, 1993, p 18). There's a real tension between the desire to reject labels and the need to affirm this thing called 'Bisexuality' as a label, as an identity upon which to build those other much-discussed (and by non-bisexuals, much-dismissed) things, a 'bisexual community', and a 'bisexual politics' (Young, 1991). When discussing the Klein Sexual Orientation Grid (a kind of more sophisticated Kinsey Scale; see Klein, Sepekoff and Wolf, 1990, p 64-81) in workshops and at meetings, many 'bisexual' people say that in an 'ideal world', they would choose not to identify as 'bisexual', since for them an ideal world would be identity- and label-free. I have trouble thinking about ideal worlds. Moreover, I think we cannot yet jettison the notion of 'bisexual identity', since, as Elisabeth Daumer has written

> "the affirmation of an integrated, unified bisexual identity, fostered within supportive bisexual communities, might boost the psychological well-being of many bisexual people". (Daumer, 1977, p 97)

Working with national and regional 'Bisexual Groups' has made this point clear to me: people need a 'home', in this far-from-ideal world of ours. More about this 'home' later, but for now I want to think more closely about what

I've just quoted from Daumer. Really her argument is about bisexuality not being a place on the margins, not being a happy hybrid identity digging away at heterosoc and homosoc; it's about a coherent, real *place* - or as I put it, a *home* - where bisexual people can belong. It might not be about a 'bisexual neighbourhood' or a 'bisexual ghetto' (now that really is incomprehensible), but it's about *community* and *identity*. Interestingly, Michael William (1993, p 38) uses the term 'bi milieu' to describe our collectivity. That seems looser, vaguer than 'community'. And he goes on to critically assess the way this milieu battles for its politics, pointing out the failings common to all 'single-issue' campaigns. From William's anarchist perspective, there's nothing to glue him together with, for example, a right-wing royalist bisexual. Nothing, that is, except their bisexuality. As Jo Eadie (1993, p 12) says, returning to the postmodern motif, there's a version of the 'bisexual community' in which "pagan transsexual lesbians share coffee with married businessmen who haven't yet come out to their wives". In short, he says, "respect for diversity has become almost - so predictably - an orthodoxy".

That's partly why a lot of bisexual people were initially very keen on the idea of 'queer'. Here at last was a dissident sexual politics we could fully be a part of - and some writers have begun to use terms like 'queer community' in an uncritically accepting way (eg Young, 1990). Or, as Elizabeth Reba Weise (1992, p xiv) optimistically puts it, "Queer politics are bi-friendly". But queer seems to have failed bisexual people, in a way, since much of what it's achieved is simply to provide a critical eye under which lesbian and gay politics and theory can be scrutinized. It's just become a postmodern, poststructuralist, post-most-things recast of 'lesbian and gay' (see Smyth (1992) for a good discussion of queer). Queer has developed its own orthodoxy, its own hierarchy of queerness (Eadie, 1993), and notions such as 'queer heterosexuality' still haven't become fully part of the queer canon, so that when Elisabeth Daumer (1992) talks about the possibility of a man and a woman having a 'lesbian relationship', she is met with a sharp intake of breath. And bisexual people have had to shout "We're Here, We're Queer, Get Used To It" not only at 'straight society', but also back at queer itself. Certainly on this side of the Atlantic, it seems as if the whole queer thing has degenerated into a battle between certain forces within (mainly male) gay culture; forces cast by their opposition as 'trendy' on one side and 'conservative' on the other. Like so many debates - essentialism versus constructionism, for example - it's become little more than a discussion-point at academic dinner parties, its radical edge blunted by all that chattering.

The Question of Home

To return now to thinking about the question of 'home', Carol Queen (1991, p 21), wrote in her essay 'The Queer In Me', that for her as a bisexual woman "home is not a place but a process". This is a significant phrase, in that it suggests the contingent and provisional nature of identities, and in particular of bisexual identities. It reminds me of Doreen Massey's (1992, p 8) comment: "That place called home was never an unmediated experience"; and of bell hooks's (1991, p 49) "home is no longer just one place. It is locations". Tim Putnam's (1993, p 150) question, "Where - and what - is home in a postmodern geography?" is also especially resonant here.

What Queen ultimately hopes to find is a (coming-out) place called home (echoed in the title of Elizabeth Reba Weise's (1992) collection on bisexuality and feminism, *Closer To Home*). Here we come back to the contradictions mentioned earlier: it's seductive to celebrate the destabilizing possibilities of conceiving of home as not fixed - but what comfort and support does that offer someone unsure about their sexual identity? Someone who wants a solid place to *come home to*, rather than a free- floating postmodern ethereal process we try to convince them is called home? Can we actually live in such a process? Is that a solid foundation on which to build?

Anne Seller, in a 'portfolio' co-written with Morwenna Griffiths (1992, p 136), discusses "'coming home' experiences", which mark "the end of uneasiness in the world, the end of dis-ease ... and the ability to recognise your 'family'". Home, then, is a vital site of emplacement, of situatedness, the space for living a politics of location. Neil Smith's 'scaling exercise' (1993, p 104) notes that "although the scale of the body defines the site of personal identity, the scale of the home provides the most immediate context within which this takes place". 'Home' in this sense thus contains some strains of essentialism, of being the place to 'be oneself'. Coming home thus marks the end of a journey, a quest, to 'find oneself'. This idea seems to clash with other notions about identity, about its fluidity, which abound in bisexual narratives.

Fluidity and diversity are perhaps the twin orthodoxies of bisexuality. They also imply a kind of marginality which fixed, stable identities don't have. Fluidity in sexual choices has to an extent become essentialised as part of the 'everyone's bisexual really' school of bi-theorizing (eg Himelhoch, 1990). This seems an entirely unhelpful (but very common) way of thinking about bisexuality, despite arguments stressing anti-essentialist viewpoints (eg Udis-Kessler, 1990). But here we go again, theorizing away essentialism, while at the same time remembering how many people believe in it (and thinking about how a conference paper which talked about identities as 'necessary fictions' was received by activists who didn't want to be told their struggles were for nothing more than fictions). Arguments about the 'strategic deployment' of essentialism (eg Fuss, 1989; Rose, 1993) are worth noting here.

Jo Eadie (1992, p 6) has talked about what he punningly called "the epistemology of the fence" - in reaction to the common charge that bisexual people are uncommitted, undecided fence-sitters. The fence, like the slash separating hetero and homo, occupies a disruptive position, cleaving the other two (in both senses of the word). This helps, as Elisabeth Daumer (1992, p 98) says, "shed light on the gaps and contradictions of all identity, on what we might call the difference *within* identity [as well as *between* identities]". The fence can thus be a good place to sit, since the 'postmodern' strand of bisexual theorizing must echo Judith Butler's (1990, p vii) conclusion that "trouble is inevitable and the task, how best to make it, what best way to be in it". Learning to love the fence, perhaps that's the secret of *How To Be a Happy Bisexual* (with no apologies to that great biphobe Terry Sanderson). But can we really live on a fence? Isn't trying to live there always going to be a precarious balancing act. You can never relax, or you might fall off. But what other homes are open to us?

At Home He Feels Like A Tourist

One accusation raised against bisexual people by the lesbian and gay community is that we are simply 'tourists', taking trips into 'gay' subcultures, having our fun, then going home with a few snapshots and some fond memories. This is an interesting metaphor, one of a number which constructs us as fundamentally heterosexual people who dabble in a bit of same-sex activity now and again (Evans, 1993). We go on trips to sample exotic pleasures like businessmen in Bangkok. In this kind of discourse our true 'home' is heterosoc (since it's based on a model of bisexual people as living with heterosexual privilege and just flirting with homosexuality - thus ignoring those bisexuals who are in same-sex relationships, in no relationships, or in more complex affectional configurations), rather than the fence between it and homosoc. And of course for many people who have desires for both sexes heterosoc is home, because the fence is so damn uncomfortable and homosoc so unwelcoming. But it must always be remembered that we are not just sex-tourists having our fun in the gay sun, sending our postcards from the edge; heterosoc is not the home we want to be in. It's one of the homes we are put into by other people.

The other home we are put into is the gay and lesbian milieu. To many people, we are 'really gay/lesbian', but just too scared or fucked up to admit it. That's why we totter around on the margins - we are too frightened to jump into the centre, forever wallflowers. As an interesting twist to this locating of bisexuality within a 'gay home', a recent booklet co-produced by London Lesbian and Gay Switchboard and SM Gays, entitled *Rough Sex, Safer Sex* included information on 'specialist activities' of (mainly) gay men, such as rimming, watersports, scat, fisting - and bisexuality. Adverts in the gay press for telephone chatlines and sexlines also frequently lump bisexuality (or as they are apt to put it, Bi-guys and Bi-girls) in with other 'specialist' categories, and there have been a smattering of pieces in the gay press which have discussed bisexuality in this way: the following quotation is taken from the 'A to Z of Sex' section of the British gay freesheet *Boyz*, probably the trashiest, least PC publication currently rolling off the pink press:

G IS FOR GIRLS

Intellectual queens spend a lot of time discussing whether or not we should 'deconstruct our sexuality'. What they're going on about is whether it's politically correct for boys with a gay identity to have sex with girls.
Well, a lot of boys who mainly sleep with boys often have sex with girls, too. And as far as I can see it's quite OK, natural and wonderful that they do. Girls are good to have sex with too, or so I'm told...   ('Boyzdoc' Matthew Helbert, 1993, p 18)

Although this quote has some notable shortcomings (it doesn't actually mention the B-word, instead talking of 'boys with a gay identity'; and note how the author distances himself from 'sleeping with girls'), it is nevertheless one of the most matter-of-fact handlings of 'bisexuality' I've ever seen in the gay (sic) press, although it follows the Rough Sex, Safer Sex formula of making bisexuality a 'specialist activity' of some gays and lesbians, rather than a valid sexuality in its own right.

So perhaps it's not surprising that many people who find that they are attracted to the 'same sex' as well as the 'opposite sex' are willing to leap right into the gay club and declare themselves absolutely bent (but with a bit of a kink). They've found their home, washed that man or woman right out of their hair and 'become' a dyke or a faggot. But what's left for those of us who don't want to wash our hair that clean? Who want to love men and women? Where can we go to let our (unwashed) hair down with whoever we choose? What has the bi milieu, shakily perched on the margin/fence, managed to build for us?

The introduction to *Closer to Home* lists the achievements of the bi milieu in the States, creating a network, some might even say a community, that is becoming increasingly visible, strong and proud. And here in Britain, too, things are developing, with conferences, local groups, political bodies, magazines and books, and a constant nagging for representation and inclusion (Bell, 1992). There's still an awful lot of biphobia to cut through, but some things are changing for the better. Certainly, there are too many of us causing too much trouble to be deemed nonexistent. Hopefully.

More Trouble

One last thing that bisexuality obviously troubles is the relationship between sex, gender and desire; something which so-called monosexual constructs do not challenge. It thus enters into Gayle Rubin's (1989, p 282) domain of "scary sex" - sex which is scary because it is troublesome. In this way bisexual identity, and bisexual politics, are equally scary. By saying that gender isn't a fundamental criterion in choosing your object of desire, bisexuality effects a very scary, a very troubling, erasure. Here again a lot of bisexual thinking is clotted up with banal aphorisms along the lines of "I don't love men and women, I love people". This idea seems to belong to that label-free ideal world mentioned earlier. But the very notion of not using a genital definition of one's love and sex choices certainly has disruptive potential for throwing light on the constructedness of gender and of sex. If, as Paula Rust (1992, p 305) suggests, we could cease to see "partner sex" as the way of defining sexuality, then "observers would no longer be able to see heterosexuality and homosexuality any more than they can now see bisexuality". This leads Rust onto a new term, "pansensuality", rather like the "fully sexual" mentioned earlier. For Rust, pansensuality upholds the same utopian vision that queer might once have done.

So, bisexual, pansensual, fully sexual, queer ... ultimately, what's in a name? Paula Rust (1992, p 306) again: "all political movements challenge the status quo by naming themselves". Naming is the first step towards identity, and politics, and community. By naming we lay claim to a home. While the whole notion of identity politics has rightly been interrogated, there's something ... comforting, if you like, about being named. Something to do with the 'well-being' of 'belonging', perhaps. I was going to call this chapter 'Bisexuality: a place on the margins, or a *new centre?*' but I decided that was far too elegiac, too much like those ideal-world slogans. I don't want to privilege bisexuality - since that too reeks of essentialism, utopianism, and ultimately of myopism - but neither do I want to uncritically celebrate marginality. All I want is to look at the things bisexuality does to our ways of thinking. To look at the trouble it causes. And how that trouble can begin to expose all the complexities, contradictions and compromises which make up all sexual identities. I agree with Elisabeth Daumer (1992) when she says that attempts to construct a bisexual identity do not always bear out their radical potential - which leads her on to favouring queer (and here I'd like to point out that Daumer's version of queer is an inclusive and very positive one, which would "stress the interrelatedness of different, and at times conflicting, communities and thus emphasize the need to combine forces in our various antihomophobic and antisexist endeavours" (Daumer, 1992: 103)). But then, bearing out radical potential - being a troublemaker, making the margin a home - that isn't what everyone wants. I hope my own troubled discussions of the tensions and contradictions of bisexuality have shown this, and have also managed to tread that line between celebration and commiseration that I opened with.

Bibliography

Bell, D. (1992) "The map of sexual identities - a space for bisexuality?", *Praxis* No. 24.

Bell, D. (1993) *The trouble with bisexuality*, paper presented at the 'Traces, Margins, Journeys' conference, Canterbury, February.

Bennett, K. (1992) "Feminist bisexuality: a both/and option in an either/or world", in Reba Weise, E. (ed.) *Closer To Home: bisexuality and feminism*, Seal Press, Seattle.

Bordo, S. (1992) "Postmodern subjects, postmodern bodies", *Feminist Studies*, Vol.
18.

Butler, J. (1990) *Gender Trouble: feminism and the subversion of identity*, Routledge, London.

Butler, J. 1991) "Imitation and gender insubordination", in Fuss, D. (ed) *Inside/Out: lesbian theories, gay theories*, Routledge, New York.

Daumer, E. (1992) "Queer ethics; or, the challenge of bisexuality to lesbian ethics", *Hypatia*, Vol. 7.

Eadie, J.(1992) *The Motley Crew: what's at stake in the production of bisexual identity* paper presented at the Sexuality and Space Network conference, Lesbian and Gay Geographies?, London, September.

Eadie, J. (1993) "We should be there bi now", *Rouge*, No. 12

Evans, D. (1993) *Sexual Citizenship: the material construction of sexualities*, Routledge, London.

Fuss, D. (1989) *Essentially Speaking: feminism, nature and difference*, Routledge, London.

Griffiths, M. & Seller, A. (1992) "The politics of identity: the politics of self", *Women: a cultural review*, Vol. 3.

Helbert, M. (1993) "Boyzdoc'- G is for girls", *Boyz*, 1st May.

Himelhoch, B. (1990) "The bisexual potential", in Geller, T. (Ed) *Bisexuality: a reader and sourcebook*, Times Change Press, Ojai.

hooks, b. (1991) *Yearning: race, gender, and cultural politics*, Turnaround, London.

Jackson, P. (1993) "Visibility and voice", *Environment and Planning D: Society and Space*, Vol. 11.

Jarman, D. *At Your Own Risk: a saint's testament*, Hutchinson, London.

Klein, F., Sepekoff, B. & Wolf, T. (1990) "Sexual orientation: a multi-variable dynamic process", in Geller, T. (ed) *Bisexuality: a reader and sourcebook*, Times Change Press, Ojai.

Massey, D. (1992) "A place called home?", *New Formations*, Vol. 17

McDowell, L. (1992) "Multiple voices: speaking from inside and outside 'the project'", *Antipode*, Vol. 24.

Pink Dandelion, B. (1992) "Bisexual or not?", *Bifrost*, No. 20.

Putnam, T. (1993) "Beyond the modern home: shifting the parameters of residence", in Bird, J., Curtis, B., Putnam, T., Robertson, G. & Tickner, L. (eds) *Mapping the Futures: local cultures, global changes*, Routledge, London.

Queen, C. (1991) "The queer in me", in Hutchins, L. and Kaahumanu, L. (eds) *Bi Any Other Name: bisexual people speak out*, Alyson, Boston.

Rough Sex, Safer Sex (undated booklet produced by London Lesbian & Gay Switchboard and SM Gays).

Rubin, G. (1989) "Thinking sex: notes for a radical theory of the politics of sexuality", in Vance, C. (ed) *Pleasure and Danger: exploring female sexuality*, Pandora, London.

Rust, P. (1992) "Who are we and where do we go from here? Conceptualizing bisexuality", in Reba Weise, E. (Ed) *Closer To Home: bisexuality and feminism*, Seal Press, Seattle.

Smith N. (1993) "Homeless/global: scaling places", in Bird, J., Curtis, B., Putnam, T., Robertson, G. & Tickner, L. (eds) *Mapping the Futures: local cultures, global changes*, Routledge, London.

Smith, S. (1987) *A Poetics of Women's Autobiography: marginality and the fictions of self-representation*, Indiana University Press, Bloomington.

Smyth, C. (1992) *Lesbians Talk Queer Notions*, Scarlet Press, London.

Udis-Kessler, A. (1990) "Bisexuality in an essentialist world", in Geller, T. (ed) *Bisexuality: a reader and sourcebook*, Times Change Press, Ojai.

William, M. (1993) "Bisexuality", *Anarchy: a journal of desire armed*, No. 13.

Young, S. (1990) *Bisexual, lesbian (and gay) community, and the limits of identity politics*, paper presented at the 4th annual Lesbian, Bisexual and Gay Studies Conference, Cambridge MA, October.

Young, S. (1991) *Bisexual theory and the postmodern dilemma, or, what's in a name*, paper presented at the 5th annual Lesbian and Gay Studies conference, New York, November.

8 Sex in the margins

Wouter Geurtsen

Abstract

A repression of 'abnormal' sexualities in the United Kingdom is evident. One of the consequences is the disappearance of cultures of so-called sexual deviants from normal, everyday life as the marginalised culture goes underground. This disappearance, this non-visibility, will have a feedback effect on the mis/understanding of sexual diversity, sexual cultures, sexual identities and sexual lifestyles. The combination of misunderstanding, absence from everyday life and political repression of sexual cultures, can be typified as a negative climate for people to come to terms with their sexual desires on the one hand and will make it more difficult to learn a culture of safer sex on the other. This inhibition on self-regulation of sexual behaviour within a scene through outside repression is undesirable and dangerous for HIV prevention.

This chapter will focus on the SM (sadomasochism)-gay scene as an example of this mechanism. It is based on a comparative post graduate research on the SM-gay-scenes in Amsterdam and London.

After the ending of the 1950's witch hunt against homosexuals, and the resultant legal reforms introduced by Wolfenden in 1967, at least part of the harsh repression of gay life was lifted in the United Kingdom (although numerous discriminating measures still exist). In the decades thereafter, this climate proved to be liberal enough for the commercial gay scene to develop. Part of this scene is the SM-gay-scene, often referred to as the leatherscene. This scene is the cultural product of processes of modernisation, which started with small and relatively sealed off groups of gay men involved in sadomasochistic practices which formed in the post- war period.

The groups grew steadily, became more open to outsiders and increased contact with others, throughout the 1960's and 1970's.

In the second half of the eighties however, HIV and AIDS came on the gay scene and had profound ambiguous transforming effects on it and on SM in general. As will be demonstrated, the fight against AIDS on the scene will improve considerably if both politicians and HIV-prevention workers will really take into account the culture of safer sex which has developed at the core of the gay scene. Operation Spanner, the latest legal action against SM, which is not discussed extensively in this paper, is in this context an excellent example of how things should not be[1].

History of the SM Culture of Gay Men

In many cases, the origins of the SM-gay scene are traced back to the second World war. Guy Baldwin, describing the American scene, explains the way gay veterans who were used to a homosocial environment got involved with the biker/SM culture upon their return to the States:

> Upon their return to the States about 1946, many of the gay vets wanted to retain the most satisfying elements of their military experience and, at the same time, hang out socially and sexually with other masculine gay men. They found that only in the swashbuckling motorcycle culture did such opportunities exist and so the gay bike clubs were born. (Baldwin, G. 1991)

Leather, rough sex and rules about dominance and submission were part of this very masculine gay culture, and avoidance of contact with effeminate men was part of the rules of inclusion and exclusion described by Baldwin. In later stages, he states that:

> .... kinky people have segregated themselves out from the riders as the process of erotic specialisation has continued. (Baldwin, G. 1991)

A segregation which left its traces in style. Early on, the original biker-chaps had the zips on the outside to avoid the scratching of the motorbike, but afterwards, when leather became more and more fashionable among the gay crowd, they disappeared to the inside because it looked better.

Gay men who were involved in sadomasochistic practices felt at ease with being leathermen, which offered them an identity, a network of like minded people and a style which offered enough opportunities for erotic fantasies and fetishes. But to be clear, SM in those early days, in the States as well as in the UK, was cloak and dagger work. It was not permitted in a society which didn't even allow for consensual homosexual contacts to exist. SM took place in private within a very small circle of friends. They would arrive at someone's house in business-suits, change there into their leather gear, have a session in outfit and change clothes back again before leaving. It had to remain a secret. One respondent told me that:

> If people would find out that we were having homosexual contacts, we would be sent to jail. If they would find out that we were involved in SM, the key would be thrown away.'[2]

Older respondents, as well as heavy SM-ers, make a distinction between the modern leatherscene, revolving around fashion and style, and the SM scene which is more private and centred around perverse sexual practices.

The repressive climate for SM sex resulted in a strict self-regulation of sex and partners within these circles. It was very hard to get into these circles as an outsider, and the people within these circles generally didn't have a lot of sex outside it. The consequences of this mode of self-regulation will be dealt with later on within the context of HIV prevention.

The masculine style of the leatherscene proved to be very successful among the gay crowd of the sixties and seventies. The leatherscene grew fast, became more wide spread and more commercial. It was not centred around voluntary associations such as the bikers organisation but around bars. The attraction of the leather culture extended to the group of gay men who like to be butch, but who are not necessarily into SM. These men are usually referred to as 'clones', due to their uniform appearance consisting of flat top, moustache, plaid and checked shirt, jeans and construction boots.

The leather scene, during its commercialisation and growth, became more open and visible in the main cities of Western societies. Travel from one area of the gay scene to another increased. Bars had dark rooms - if allowed - in which one could have anonymous sex. Specific commercial enterprises and magazines started to cater specifically this scene.

The Impact of HIV and AIDS on the Scene

The high level of national and international interaction between the local SM-gay-scenes, which is also notable on the plain level of sexual intercourse, made these scenes a suitable network for the HIV virus to spread. No wonder AIDS hit hard within the scene. Anonymous, heavy and unprotected sex belonged to the sociocultural pattern of the scene:

> Erotic patterns .... included cruising and tricking. .... A rough, uninhibited phallocentric form of sexuality characterized tricking among clones. Tricking frequently involved 'deep throating', 'Hard fucking', and 'heavy tit work'. .... Most tricks consisted

of a single erotic encounter. That is, the men had sex once and never again. (Levine, M. 1992)

According to one of my interviewees, clone culture:

(...) was the culture that was worst affected by AIDS whether you are looking at Amsterdam or London. It was clone culture. And it was clone culture which travelled on the cheap, first cheap transatlantic flights in the mid 70's, the American flights. So that first and second generation of people with AIDS in Amsterdam and London and Paris, in my experience, were very similar men. My age, a bit older, a bit younger, almost all of them plaid shirts, blue jeans, a moustache, flat tops. All of them have been in Earl's Court in this town. ..... That culture is the Tom of Finland culture, you see. That was the culture that was about fast fuck.[3]

Before a culture of safer sex developed in the scene from the mid-eighties onwards, an obvious reaction to AIDS was to stop having sex within the scene, to leave the city or to couple up. When the owner of a prominent leather club in London was asked about the effect HIV and AIDS had on his club, he answered:

Originally, devastating. People didn't want to be seen going out to clubs, to leather bars or whatever, because it was assumed that people on the leatherscene were doing everything unsafely and people lost interest in sex. And the club-scene generally took a nose-dive. It was awful. And then people started realising that you can have sex without having any risk, you can go out to clubs. So things started going back up, and now we seem to have dealt with that and we are not doing too badly. People want to enjoy clubbing again.
(I) : Did a lot of people leave the scene because of AIDS?'
A lot of people left London. A lot of people moved out to the south coast, Brighton and Bournemouth.'[4]

So, in the beginning, on the consumption-side the leather scene became quieter. But this also happened on the production-side:

.... people just wouldn't be to be associated with clubs like ours. .... Everybody assumed that it was, to start with, it was only people on that scene that were going to catch the disease because they were the one's that appeared to have the most sex,

146

you know. So a lot of places .... on the leather scene .... changed
and tried to get more 'normal' people in.

It is not just that the bars and clubs on the leather scene disappeared
because they wanted to change their image or because the number of their
clients went down. In San Francisco for instance, the closing down of the
leather bars in Folsom Street is also related to the economic and geographical
re-structuring of this previously marginal area which pushed the bars out
because the rents became too expensive.

The changes mentioned above are autonomous changes of the leather scene
itself. But certain changes which occurred in the place the scene occupies
within gay culture are also significant, although they are often paradoxical
in their effects. It is a contraction in which the scene is relatively closed off
from input from young people but a lot of older people still frequent it.

When the relative high average age of the scene is kept in mind together
with the high level of infection, it is understandable - though by no means
to be condoned - that a lot of non-scene people (especially younger gay men
who have come out after the AIDS crisis), blame the leather scene for it. If
you are an older gay man, this results in feeling even more out of place in
the bars and clubs where the youngsters go to. Turning to the leather crowd
is in this situation one possible solution for gay men over thirty:

> I think ..... that leather or fetishistic sex has, the role has
> changed and has become more popularised, but also more
> marginalised...
> [I] : How do you mean that?
> Well, I think that generally speaking and this is only a
> generalisation, so don't quote me (as) absolute. People who are
> into fetish, or any other sort of description, leather or whatever,
> tend to be...Well, gay men tend to sort of graduate to that, and
> it tends to be sort of roundabout the age of 30, people tend to
> graduate into fetishism. And there is not really a mix between
> the leather or fetishistic scene and the non-leather scene. In fact,
> there is a great deal of antipathy between the two. And so, I
> think that that has got something to do with AIDS, because I
> think a lot of younger gay men tend to see the generation above
> them as somehow a reservoir of infection ..... Well, I think this
> is totally wrong, but people have these perceptions ..... And I
> think that has resulted in a kind of separation process ..... I think
> when you reach 30, one seems to be over the hill..... And one
> of the few places where you can break out of the rigid
> perceptions of sexuality, is by joining the leather/fetish scene.
> Because that's a role they can get into. It is a sort of

consumerist market. It .... is a factor for gay men to find a sexuality, particularly for older gay men. I mean, there are some younger gay men who do go to leather clubs like the Block ...., but very often the sort of age range begins to start about 28, 29, 30 and goes right up to 50 and in some cases 60. So it really is sort of, where queens go when they turn 30, they go to leather clubs. Because if you don't go to leather clubs, everywhere else is very young. It is sort of 18, 19 years old. And I think it is very real and very palpable.[5]

Another man, who is over thirty years old, not into SM but who does go to the leather bars, said about non-scene bars in an interview:

But you get other pubs, when you go to them, they're all young, and when you are over a particular age, when you are over twenty-eight, you feel completely out of place. And if you do try and act young, you're gonna be ending up looking like a complete idiot. You know, like jumping around on a floorboard for 3 hours and in the end of it, you have to have some oxygen, because you are knackered.[6]

Incidentally, he told me he knows twenty-eight people with AIDS personally. No wonder he sounds rather bitter.

This contraction-process works on the other side as well. Older men are often valued as potential sexual partners in the leather-scene for their (supposed) sexual experience, whereas the youngsters in that scene are often refused by older men, most notably by masters, because of their unreliability in keeping appointments for sexual sessions and in sustaining sexual relations over a longer period.

So far, I have looked at the consequences of HIV and AIDS for the leather scene. This all amounts to a quite negative picture: the people on the leather scene have died, they moved out, places closed down or became quieter in the first few years of the AIDS-crisis - the scene contracted. (Also, and this is not specific for the leatherscene, the decline in free disposable income due to the ongoing economic depression in the UK, stops people going out very often.) Does this all mean that SM and leather - or fetishism in general - are ultimately going to disappear from gay culture? No, because at the same time as the increase in HIV and AIDS, the interest in leather and fetish has increased in contemporary culture, as a whole and in urban gay culture in particular. What has happened, and is still happening, is that people are looking for safe and erotic alternatives to penetrative sex and finding it in fetish dressing:

I would say there is a lot more people who are into getting dressed up. There is a lot more people into shaving. There is a lot more people into piercing as well. They have rings in their nipples, their ears, their nose or whatever places, at the end of their dicks.

[I] : Do you think there is a link between fetishism and HIV and AIDS?

You mean saying has fetishism and SM increased because of HIV and AIDS, is that the question that you are asking me? .... I think there is. Because you can have a very exciting, stimulating variation to the purely penetrative gay sex, which is essentially very safe with respect to HIV and AIDS. .... Certainly a lot of fetish dressing is totally safe.

[I] : It seems to me that fetishism is now much more out in the open. Have you got an idea why it is?

I think on the basis, actually, it has to do with safer sex, with using your imagination and doing things you would thought of, as a alternative to have a .. fuck, a fuck basically.[7]

Besides the motivation to explores fetishism because of HIV and AIDS, it is possible that a lot of people are starting to use fetishism because it has become much more acceptable and available in main stream culture. These two changes are probably interrelated. The main recent example of fetishism (and also SM) becoming more publicly available is the book *Sex* by Madonna. It is interesting that a lot of hard core SM'ers dislike it because the bondage gear etc. in her book looks very pretty but is not very functional. Her leather hand cuffs for instance, will break quickly if they are used for restraint in a heavy corporal punishment (CP) session. But nevertheless, contemporary culture is currently promoting fetish and SM. I asked my interviewee quoted above, whom I interviewed together with his business partner, to expand about the increasing interest in fetishism:

[I] : Do you think the fact that fetishism has come out in the open has to do with AIDS / HIV?

I think on the gay scene, yeah. I think also that in terms where contemporary culture is at, you see a lot around, *Batman* films and things like that. It is, the second *Batman* film, is about fetish. It is about, forget the plot, it's about fetish. It's about childhood trauma, about sexuality, dressing up and playing power games. And trying to solve, to relate, the bit that wants to be caring and loving and tendered, that bit that wants to trash the hell out of each other. .... And so there have two things happened; there is safer sex and then there is a contemporary fashion floatation, with at this moment Vivienne Westwood is again producing bondage stuff, you know, it will fade away. But there is obviously a bigger thing underlying serious fetish scene ..... There are more places where people can use their imagination more. And in terms of the press-media saying, yes, it's okay, it's fun, do it. Along with the sort of debate about how healthy it is and should we getting into role playing. Now it is like, Yes, go for it .... Forget how wrapped up it is, save your lives.[8]

SM always had an element of fetishism incorporated in it and there are a number of reasons to believe that SM also has gained impetus under the impact of HIV and AIDS. First, SM can be in itself safe sex. A lot of SM practices do not involve the exchange of body fluids. Secondly, a lot of SM sessions, for instance bondage or CP, are not orgasm centred. And thirdly, in the negotiation process before engaging in a consensual SM session that has always existed, the issue of HIV and AIDS could be incorporated quite easily when compared to the relatively spontaneous script of sexual contacts in non-SM circles.

So, regardless of the changing place of the leather-scene in gay urban culture, there are quite a number of reasons to become involved in SM and fetishism, which are related to a changing perception of SM and fetishism in (gay) sexuality because of the consequences of HIV and AIDS in contemporary culture. But why then is it that the fetish scene is becoming more popular than the leather scene? There certainly is no definite answer to this, but one impression is that it is related, again, to contemporary culture. Is it postmodernity? Perhaps. The interviewee who is quoted above about modern culture was also questioned about this issue, though indirectly. His answer denotes the difference between the prototype visitors of both scenes:

[I] : Do you think that the traditional master and slaves-relationships belong more to the past, and that fetishism is more something of the nineties?
No, it doesn't. I think the serious masters and slaves will always be there. The modern fetish groupee will put more the emphasis on dressing up, exhibiting himself and he may be beaten for one night and then, going home, rubbing their bottom and thinking: "No, I don't like that, I don't want to do that any more".[9]

After which his partner declares his preference for the fetish-scene:

But about the relation between sadomasochism and fetishism, fucking someone with their socks on is my favourite example of something that is fetishistic, but is completely run away from whips, chains, masters and slaves. And I think the SM, the master and slave scene is an aspect of fetish, and now it is gone bhammm, it has expanded. And I don't like leather, I like plastic. I don't like pain, I like sensuality. I don't like controlling someone, I like exhibiting myself. So it can be clean, fun, jolly, but still be fetishistic and get a kick out of it.[10]

The Culture of Safer Sex

It has been demonstrated already that AIDS has had ambiguous effects on the SM scene. Besides, the very negative impact through illness and death on the one hand and through the abandonment of old sexual routines on the other, AIDS also increased interest in SM or, put more correctly, in fetishism. But there is more to it than that. A culture of safer sex has developed within the scene, encompassing a set of cultural practices which are about HIV risk reduction. The question of safety is solved by a set of finely tuned rules and practices which makes it unnecessary in everyday sexual contacts to refer explicitly to the safety of sexual practices. It is a soft self regulating safety practice. When two people well informed by this culture get in touch with each other, they don't need to halt the erotic encounter and say 'stop, I want it safe' (or whatever) to keep it that way (the rough and touch safety practice promoted heavily by HIV prevention workers); it is ensured through finer mechanisms acquired through experience.

I want to deal first with the parameters of this discussion before getting into it. In the first place, it can be placed within the context of postmodernity. It is a discussion about the reduction of ambiguity and insecurity presently prominent in post-modern Western societies (Giddens 1992).

Secondly, there is no uniform quality about this so-called culture of safer sex. An important distinction within this discussion is between the core and the periphery of the scene. It is mainly in the periphery of the scene that people are not informed about risks and their reductions. But the core is well informed. AIDS has taken such a prominent place in their lives - usually they know people with HIV - that they will make sure they will only have safer sex. So, (to put it bluntly) they won't fuck without a condom, they won't use condoms unsuitable for anal sex and they will use water based lubricants. It is mainly in the periphery of the scene that mistakes are still made, which has to be taken into account in the HIV prevention discussion.

Another distinction is the one between the so-called old guard and the new people on the scene. Within the old guard, the group of people who were on the scene a long time before HIV and AIDS existed, different strategies can be found. Remember, for them SM was cloak and dagger work. Solutions to the problem of safety can be found in that direction:

> .... we didn't play safe as you would call it safe nowadays. We very rarely used condoms, and eh, we had no inhibitions about oral sex. Semen was taken quite willingly, piss was taken quite willingly, and we're not infected by the main stream hiv infection. 'Cause we didn't mix in that circle. Our circles are closed circles, and we didn't have sex outside those circles. Or, if we did, which was very rare, and we were also very careful who we had sex with.
>
> I have three slaves. We have been together now, the longest slave I have is three and a half years, the second two and a half years, and the third one a year and a half. We all trust each other. We all talk about this quite openly and intimately. We all have had hiv-tests ..... Now, we don't live the life of monks. We do have sex outside our circle. But if we have sex outside our circle, we play 100% safe. Within our circle, we do not practice 100% safe sex because we trust each other, and the tests have been negative all along the line. So ...., I fuck one of my slaves anally without a condom. But he has no other sex partner at all. Because if he had, I would know about it.[11]

This is a risk reduction strategy which puts very high demands on the inter-personal relationship between the partners in order for them to have sex without worry. A strategy suitable only for those, who emphasise the connection between sex and long term emotional engagement between partners, which is a connection made more easily by the old guard because of the hidden nature of SM in times of serious repression.

The culture of safer sex referred to earlier is more prominent within the young (and not so young) crowd in the core scene. Recreational sex with unknown partners is a regular practice among them. Usually they are aware of all the information about risks and safer sex. To my astonishment however, they often tell when interviewed, that when they engage in a trick, they do not refer explicitly to safer sex. Does this mean that they don't care whether to have sex safely or not? No. Safe sex is the standard:

I just told you about those two real drunk men fucking each other [without a condom, W.G.]. That has been the only incident I've ever seen in the five years I go a lot to darkrooms... And eh... If you consider the fact that I've had hundreds of contacts, and no one proposed to get fucked without a condom or other dangerous things, well, I think, it is safe .... So, I always did tell for a while, when I started playing with someone, you have eye-contact, there has been a bit of touching and things like that, and one of the first things I did was to tell them that I wanted it safe. I did that for half a year, and eh, the answer was always yes, of course .... Now I rarely mention it. Usually you can feel it, you sense that well, this boy eh, it is clear that eh... He'll do it safe.[12]

The culture of safer sex is taken for granted. It outs itself in a intuition people have that a partner will keep it safe also. It is therefore a very hidden and often neglected feature amongst others, including HIV prevention workers and politicians. They tend to neglect this very important feature of risk reduction and do not promote it. The fact that safety often is not a prominent issue darkrooms, only makes them worried. Politicians in this context seek solutions in repression, the closing down of opportunities to have anonymous sex on the scene. HIV prevention workers deal with it through the production and distribution of even more posters and leaflets about safer sex.

Both parties would be well advised to give second thoughts to their policies. Wouldn't it be wiser to create a sphere of openness about anonymous sex instead of repressing it, thereby promoting the consumption of sex through which the culture of safer sex is becoming more shared and wide spread? Are HIV-prevention workers really aware of the consequences of the culture of safer sex? If people feel they know about risks and reductions, they will not read and absorb the written information produced by them. The promotion of safety in the scene can be improved considerably by the formation of so-called affinity groups, in which core members of the scene engage with and inform newcomers about the ways to have safe sex.

But, to end with, an open climate about sexuality is quintessential for the development of the culture of safer sex. The de-criminalisation of SM and of non-private gay sexuality must come first and foremost in the quest to save lives. British policies, with such features as the recent Operation Spanner (the criminalisation of SM under the 1861 Offences Against the Person Act, not discussed in this chapter) have to change.

Endnotes

1. A discussion about Operation Spanner can be found in Paul Geerts and Wouter Geurtsen (1993).

2. Source: interview dd. 8-6-1993.

3. Source: interview dd. 22-11-1992.

4. Source: interview dd. 10-7-1992.

5. Source: interview dd. 14-8-1992.

6. Source: interview dd. 10-7-1992.

7. Source: interview dd. 10-7-1992.

8. Source: interview dd. 31-7-1992.

9. Source: interview dd. 31-7-1992.

10. Source: interview dd. 31-7-1992.

11. Source: interview dd. 8-6-1993.

12. Source: interview dd. 8-5-1993.

Bibliography

Baldwin, Guy. (1991) "Old Guard; Its Origins, Mystique and Rules", *Drummer* 150, Desmodus Incorporation, San Francisco.

Geerts, P., Geurtsen, W. (1993) "Celstraf voor bondage en spanking; Engelse justitie opent klopjacht op SM-ers", *XL* Mei 1993 pp 28-29.

Giddens, A. (1992) *The Transformation of Intimacy*, Cambridge University Press, Cambridge.

Levine, M. P. (1992) "The Life and Death of Gay Clones", Herdt, G. (ed.) *Gay Culture in America; Essays From the Field*. Beacon Press, Boston Massachusetts.

R v Brown, *CR App Reports*, 1992.

9 The twilight world of the sadomasochist

Jon Binnie

I had originally intended to write a chapter about sadomasochism and space. Yet when I began writing, I became troubled by how I would actually present this work, and represent SM in particular. So what follows are my reflections on doing research on sexuality within the space of academic geography. I don't claim to have any conclusive answers to the questions and issue I raise. My main aim here is open up a constructive debate around sexuality in the research process.

Sadomasochism: Shock Horror Stories

Throughout the early Summer of 1993, the homophobic murder of five gay men in London led to a media spectacle focusing on the "gay killer". The focus in the media turned on gay men as (self) oppressors, rather than as victims of homophobic crimes. The press ran sensationalist stories on the London SM scene exploring what they termed "The Twilight World of the Sadomasochist". Journalists descended on the Coleherne - London's best-established leather bar to uncover horror stories of the sordid dark reality of gay SM. The British tabloid press are the enemy one knows and are generally utterly predictable in the way they operate. Less predictable (and therefore more frightening in my view) are others within the Academy and their representation of sex in general and SM in particular. There are inevitably constraints in writing about these subjects in academic contexts, as elsewhere as they are deemed 'sensitive', and 'controversial'. There is an immediate knee jerk reaction at the prospect of being confronted with something one doesn't understand, and which may challenge simplified perceptions of reality. Writing about sexuality means censorship from the outside as well as considerable self-censorship. I have been rather bemused by how others perceive me and my research, and equally more than a little concerned about how I would present this work to others. I acknowledge the need to solicit interest in my work while simultaneously avoiding the dangers of being seen as an exotic creature. One treads a fine line between being open and responsive to curiosity and pandering to the deeply voyeuristic heterosexual gaze.

How does one present an accurate and balanced, yet critical analysis of SM given the dominant sexuality's phobic representation of SM (and in Britain) the criminalisation of SM through Operation Spanner? (It is not my intention here to explore the full implications of Operation Spanner for sexual citizenship in Britain. This has been done elsewhere (see Bell, 1993; Bibbings and Alldridge, 1993; Cooper, 1993)). The highly polarised nature of 'SM debate' within feminism also means that there is little space for any intelligent discussion of SM. While all the time I share a deep suspicion towards censorship, and hostility towards certain feminists such as Sheila Jeffreys for whom SM is morally reprehensible, I am also highly dubious of the more utopian claims of activists who advocate and proclaim SM sexualities as the best thing since sliced bread. Certainly SM is a convenient label for which is so under-researched and misrepresented. It is important to realise that SM remains a highly nuanced and complex intermeshing of different dynamic communities with the label SM often obscuring more than it illuminates. What I have been concerned with in my work is how these communities have changed over time and in space; specifically since the onset of the AIDS crisis. If SM is not a threat to the established social order, but rather the empty transgression of vacuous postmodern political praxis as some commentators have described it, then why is SM being criminalised in Britain? And why now? For example Linda Grant makes a rather spurious comparison between SM activism contesting Operation Spanner, and the inactivism concerning the wars in the former Yugoslavia:

> After I returned from the sexual killing fields of the Balkans, the defence of the civil liberties of those who choose to inflict pain and violence upon one another seemed a rather sick comment on our political priorities in the nineties. (Grant, 1993, p 236).

Fear and Loathing: Spaces of Revulsion and Fascination

In erstwhile 'radical' sympathetic academic milieu it is now becoming belatedly acceptable and even respectable to do work on sexuality. Indeed, if the volume of new material being published on sexuality is any indication, one could be forgiven for thinking that sexuality is 'flavour of the month'. Despite this recent blossoming of literature, one does detect a very real reluctance to speak about sex itself and deep embarrassment when sex is mentioned.

If this is true of sex generally, the speaking about SM sex often creates more than mere blushes and nervous laughter. At one conference I recently attended (where someone sitting in the audience was laughed at for posing the perfectly sincere question "but what is postmodern really?"), one paper in which SM was represented did provoke much nervous laughter (which was then further encouraged by the speaker) with the presenter's homophobic depiction of gay men's CP (corporal punishment) for the titillation of the audience. This nervous laughter made me feel very uncomfortable sitting in my plush seat. I did not have the courage to speak up as the milieu was so intimidating. The conference at The Tate Gallery has witnessed some of the leading stars and 'experts' from the world of Cultural Studies holding court on a panel stage - an intimidating sight in itself. Would they laugh at me too? I was relieved when someone, more articulate and self-assured than myself did actually dare to pose the question - "why in such a forum does the description of SM sexual acts illicit such a giggly (and phobic) response?". Why indeed? More embarrassment and nervous silence ensued - general squeamishness. Given the increasing centrality of sexuality and the body within 'mainstream' social and cultural theory why does the actual description of SM (sex) acts still illicit such squeamishness and hilarity? Why within such an eminently sophisticated and educated audience was SM still so 'laughable' and 'unspeakable'? Do they really find it so disgusting?

Sexuality in the Research Process

Two decades of Feminist research have spawned a wealth of literature on Feminist epistemologies and research methodologies. What is problematic within this literature is the oft voiced essentialist assumption that women are better at interviewing women because they share so much in common. This promotion of gender difference, whilst ignoring other differences such as class, race, nationality, sexuality has been criticised by others. However, thus far little has been written on the sexuality of the researcher and the role that sexuality may play in the research process. The most eloquent exposition of this lack is Esther Newton's powerfully argued recent essay (Newton, 1993) in which she critiques both the disembodied nature of much ethnographic research and the current vogue for self-reflexivity.

I have based my research on a series of informal, semi-structured interviews which I conducted with those involved in the London gay SM scene(s). My knowledge of and participation in the London (gay) SM scene has also shaped and structured my research. I found my respondents through a process of networking. I interviewed people I already knew, who in turn suggested others who they thought might be interesting for me to interview. Because these were mostly friends of friends an element of trust was already established. This also meant that any betrayal of trust would rebound on me. One 'informant' who was unknown to me before a mutual friend suggested I interview him ("because he loves chattering away and never stops"), has since become a close friend. Since conducting an interview with another informant (someone I had known for over a year previously) I have come to know him rather better. Since the interview we have frequently exchanged reflections and thoughts on sexuality and the city. In this way we were creating shared meanings around sexual outsiderhood in the city. These meanings are dynamic, and discussing them in interviews can and does challenge and change them. There is a lingering concern here that I may be more interested in exploiting them (both in a personal and professional capacity), fetishising them as 'informants' in a research project, rather than being concerned with their embodied subjective experiences as 'individuals', as friends. I discussed the interviews and research question with my informants at some depth post-interview. Chatting to these people post-interview it became clear that there were many things they had been stimulated to think about in terms of how they think about the way they feel in the city. They were then (re)interviewed, so that they would have an opportunity to express their ideas and comment on my work in progress. There are times when I felt that it would have been useful to have a microphone positioned in the pillow to record some of the conversations I had shared with people I had met and had sex with. I am referring to those kind of open-ended conversations (some spontaneous, others rather well-rehearsed) which typify many sexual encounters. I suppose it was not too surprising when one informant turned my 'research questions' around by asking to be asked "what are you into?" These casual pick up conversations constitute one key element in gay cruising and gay life. They are also an incredibly efficient means of finding out a lot about someone before going off with him. In SM contexts those conversations are even more significant in ascertaining what the other guy's "into" and putting him at ease and openness in speaking about one's self and sex which characterises many gay men's interactions and chat. Many of the ideas for my work have been gleamed from what I've heard, sensed, smelled and felt in the company of strangers and friends alike. Most of this, of course takes place out of shot of a microphone or tape recorder. I suppose in conducting the interviews I wanted to get down on tape some of the ideas and opinions I knew people already held. The interview setting did though give me an opportunity to set the agenda.

A number of writers have begun to address the issues of one's own sexuality both in the research, and in the writing-up of ethnography. Not surprisingly these issues are being raised by those whose sexuality doesn't conform to the 'norm' of heterosexuality. It should be clear that one thing which draws me towards my research questions are erotic attachments and

I don't see any thing intrinsically 'bad' about that. While I accept that power inequalities do exist, are created, and negotiated in field relationships as in 'real life', why proscribe 'field relationships' which are sexual? I wish others would begin to acknowledge that the squeamishness which greets mentions of sex in academic milieu, is itself highly oppressive.

Participant Observation

> Because the meanings we seek and need are usually hidden, or at least infrequent, we decipher small declarations; just one look over the shoulder, or a detail of dress, can make us sure or unsure of getting what we want. (Bartlett, 1985, p 36).

I am often struck by the number of times gay men have told me how much they enjoy watching and 'studying' other men in bars. In a certain sense we are all 'ethnographers' when we go out on the scene. Participant observation - observing and interpreting the detailed actions, demeanour of others is the key (the secret) to successful cruising. The difference for me is that it is my vocation to write it down and examine it and present it in (mostly heterosexual) academic forum.

Lost in Translation

What concerns me is how one bridges the (often huge) gaps in meaning and understanding between the academy, the classroom and the backroom. This does seem an impossible task at times, yet the need to do so seems more urgent than ever given the general level of ignorance both within the academy and the wider society. These gaps in meaning between the spaces of activism, the academy, the street and the bar (obviously spaces which are not always mutually exclusive) do often seem impossible to transcend. To use Eva Hoffman's term it would seem inevitable that much is "lost in translation" (Hoffman, 1991). In Sedgwick's narration of her participation in an Act-Up demonstration :

> The space of the demonstration was riddled, not only with acoustal sinkholes,but with vast unbridgeable gaps of meaning. It was in these gaps, or from out of them, that the force of any public protest might materialise, but into which, as well, it constantly risked dissolving. (Sedgwick, 1993, p 124).

Moreover in certain scenarios, these gaps in meaning and understanding (which have always characterised relationships with heterosexuals are similarly pervasive between and within the spaces of lesbian, gay bisexual communities, while within certain communities across sexuality in communities of (sexual) taste.

One theme running through Stewart Home's writing is a deep bemusement with the hypocrisy of 'mainstream' (alternative); (old) New Left political writing where one's individual (sexual private actions, so clearly contradict one's political (public) statements:

> The anarchists I knew said they were into polymorphous pervisity, but most were in monogamous heterosexual relationships! (i-D, 1993, p 106).

Any writing or research is never completely undertaken as a heroic individual project. What has motivated my work has been a certain insecurity about my own sexuality within the academy. What does happen when gay men try to maintain a unified presentation of self in space? Homophobia means that there very few spaces where we can simply 'be ourselves'. While one may wear football shirts at Pride, one doesn't wear "queer as fuck" T-shirts at football matches.

Speaking from the Margins

At a recent conference someone I met spoke of the merits of speaking from the margins, of using the margins as a site of resistance. I was at first confused and taken aback by this 'wooden', very 'straight' language of Cultural Geography. Of course I knew what he meant and went along with it as he was making complementary remarks about my work. The question that immediately sprung to my mind was "where else was I suppose to speak from?" I was being positioned here as marginal, yet in my paper I had in fact discussed the centrality of Eve Sedgwick's male homosocial/homosexual axiom to the constitution of modern (British) nationalism. This fed my suspicion that the 'postmodern' recovery of the 'margins' reflects a further attempt to appropriate them on the dominant culture's own terms. For example in Rob Shield's theoretically sophistical representation of Brighton (Shields, 1991) as a "place on the margins", he focuses on the "liminality of the beach" and the Bakhtinian carnivalesque world of Brighton. Yet Brighton's history (Brighton Ourstory Project, 1992) as a safe haven for sexual non-conformity scarcely merits a mention, while he does mention a quote from tabloid newspapers describing Brighton as the "AIDS Capital of Britain" (Shields, 1991). This reflects dominant discourses on AIDS where gay men are inextricably linked to AIDS. We exist as AIDS carriers, while our agency and our embodied subjectiveness are relegate to the realm of the 'unspeakable'. Moreover given the importance of the closet in structuring lesbian and gay lives then it would seem that the margins are more often spaces of powerlessness. In her introduction to "Inside/Out", Diane Fuss warns against a :

> ..... misplaced nostalgia for or romanticisation of the outside as a privileged site of radicality... To endorse a position of perpetual or even strategic outsiderhood (a position of powerlessness, speechlessness, homelessness...) hardly seems like a viable political programm, especially when, for so many gay lesbian subjects, it is less a question of political tactics than everyday lived experience. (Fuss, 1992, p 5).

In a thought-provoking recent piece (Scott, 1992), Joan Scott has critiqued the privileging of 'experience' as authority in writers speaking from the margins. These tensions are also explored elsewhere, for example in the work of Elspheth Probyn (Probyn, 1993) and in the recent set of essays (Ramazogolu, 1993) on the encounter between feminism and the work of Foucault. 'Experience' is crucial for those whose voices which have not been heard before. To provide as many different examples of lesbian and gay experience is probably not a bad idea given that there are simply so few images and representations for 'straights' to work on. In the joint authorship of a recent paper on the performance of gender in space (Bell et al, 1994), it became clear from an early stage in the writing process that we were speaking from very different positions, a fact which was reflected in our very different writing styles which became increasingly difficult to reconcile with time. My writing style was criticised for being "too subjective" and too raw an anecdotal reflection on my 'experience'. I was evidently not distanced enough from that which I was studying or representing. In writing about something I had a great amount of myself invested, it made me more prone to seeing any theoretical attack on my writing as an attack on myself. The others were rather more circumspect in declaring their respective positions and sexualities. What writing this joint piece on queer performativity, made me wonder whether there could be such a thing as a queer methodology and what would such methodology entail? The level of ignorance is generally so high that makes any recording or documenting of hidden histories and geographies invaluable. Yet there is the ever present danger of substituting one misconception or stereotype for another. For example when I used the piece on queer performativity in space (which examined gay skinheadism and lipstick lesbians) in my teaching I found that some of my students formed the mistaken impression that these were what gay men and lesbians 'looked like' today. Still I have to admit my own complicity for what the joint writing of this paper (in itself still a relatively rare piece of academic cooperation across lesbian and gay divide) demonstrated was how little I actually knew about lesbian culture and history.

Calculated Risks - Being Naive, 'Being/Becoming Oneself'

Thomas Yingling argues the recent blossoming of Lesbian and Gay Studies should not mask the difficulties and risks associated with writing about sexuality:

> ...we should not fool ourselves: to be openly gay or lesbian in the academy, to be working in gay and lesbian literature and theory... is still to find oneself all too often embattled, belittled, and un(der) employed. This growing encampment on the margin, making its foray into the center, is therefore to be acknowledged and applauded for its labour. Those not within the lesbian and gay community are not aware of how extremely hard-won even the slightest legal or social concession toward lesbian and gay rights is or how perilously fragile the gains of the last few years remain. (Yingling, quoted by Piontek, 1992, p 151).

The additional pressures one is under due to homophobia often lead to the kind of academic writing which is often turgid, opaque, inaccessible or "classy" to use Howard Becker's term.

> Whether or not some young academics and academics-in-training want to be classy, the possibility reminds us that everyone writes as someone, affects a character, adopts a persona who does the talking for them. Literary analysts know that, but seldom examine its implications for academic writing. (Becker, 1986, p 33)

Affecting characters and adopting different personas as have of course been necessary survival strategies for gay men in environments where we are often clearly made to feel unwelcome. One can not under-exaggerate the level of dishonesty and hypocrisy within society about sex, and the academy is no exception here.

> Until we are more honest about how we feel about informants we can't try to compensate for, incorporate, or acknowledge

desire and repulsion in our analysis of subjects or in our discourse about text construction. We are also refusing to reproduce one of the mightiest vocabularies in the human language. (Newton, 1993, p 16).

Scott Tucker in his brilliant essay "Gender, Fucking and Utopia", addresses the feminist debates in censorship and pornography (Tucker, 1991) by 'inserting' himself into the argument :

> When I take a cock in my ass, I am actively taking power and pleasure, not simply reproducing a passive 'femininity', and when I choose to give my partner the chief balance of power of sex, so that he strokes my cock with his asshole while I lie bound to a bed, then something is going on which is not reducible to the one word 'patriarchy'. Since certain radical feminists are fond of conflating all cocks into one patriarchal signifier named 'the phallus', and likewise reducing all forms of fucking into 'the fuck' (read Dworkin in particular), this makes reality so much simpler. (Tucker, 1991, p 16)

What I find troubling is praise for one's honesty on the one hand, and the general recognition among colleagues that yes these issues are important. Yet this discussion tends to remain on a purely theoretical level detached from the self, compared with the open manner which (as D.A. Miller claims) does tend to mark many gay men as being different from their heterosexual counterparts:

> A would be prudent silence about the other's body never means that differences between races (or classes, or gendered, including the 'neuter') cease at any moment being thought, fantasised, eroticised, spoken: it merely deprives such differences of any tradition of articulation but the most ponderous (immobilising, intractable) one engrossed by bigotry. Between that loud-mouthed discourse and frigid liberal silence, gay men of course know a kind of third term - by which I refer to that fascinated discourse on the male body informally but incessantly spoken in bars and bedrooms, between lovers or about them between friends, a discourse that with its meticulous observation and multiple fetishing - articulates the most casual cruise. (Miller, 1992, p 42).

It is the innocence of this "fascinated discourse" which others elsewhere such as Goldsby have condemned in a forthright manner as being merely the innocence of white gay men (Goldsby, 1991). While mainstream Geographers are at long last beginning to recognise that space is sexualised as well as gendered, there is still a very deep reluctance to acknowledge that if all space is sexualised, then this means the Senior Common Room as well as the backroom of a leather bar. These are both sexualised spaces, but encoded very differently.

To what extent can one maintain, acknowledge boundaries in one's life between the 'personal' and 'political', 'public' and the 'private'? What are the appropriate uses of the self in pleasure, leisure, work and play? I would emphasise that for gay men these questions are of even greater urgency given that we have tended to 'exist' in 'leisure' time which has until recently been constantly undervalued within debates on the Left. The New Left has been guilty of ignoring sexuality. Many writers are only reluctantly beginning to engage with feminism (after dismissing it in the past). But while sexuality is not made explicit within a text doesn't mean that it is altogether absent. Once example is a recent essay by Susan Willis on "hardcore subcultures" (Willis, 1993) in which she makes a number of points about the neglect of the relationship between culture and capital within the field of Culture Studies. Yet I find her dismissal of Constance Penley's work on fandom troubling - particularly as it's one rare mention of (homo) sexuality in her piece. Though I am sympathetic to Willis's concern to understand the relationship of culture to capital space, I find the absence of a discussion of sexuality in her piece quite disturbing, particularly as she is dealing with teenagehood. Furthermore, while she mentions AIDS as one factor influencing youth subcultures, "Moshing is one of the ways that teens have responded to coming of age in an era of safe sex. It provides intense body contact without intimacy" (Willis, 1993: 368), the effects of AIDS on youth subcultures remains rather understated throughout this essay. This piece seems motivated by a mother's understandable concern to comprehend her teenage daughter's preference for wearing a black bomber jacket. ("Mom, you know I don't want to be taken for a redneck"). Being a wearer of a MA1 flight jacket does not automatically transform you into a fascist.

Writing about (gay) skinheads inevitably invites confrontation and this is certainly no less true of an intellectual context. The anarchist skinhead writer Stewart Home whose books such as "Pure Mania", "Defiant Pose" and "No Pity" have inspired (and troubled) me whilst writing this thesis has had beer glasses thrown at him by left-wingers (who characteristically fail to comprehend their irony in his writing) at public readings, according to a recent interview (i-D, 106).

Constantly I am challenged by heterosexual colleagues to state my own personal relationship with (gay) skinhead culture - to come clean as it were. These colleagues, who characteristically rarely 'consciously' reveal much of themselves in their work, and assiduously avoid doing so, (rather arrogantly and voyeuristically in my view) believe they have a right to know everything about you and dictate to you how to live your life. They continue to write in a disembodied, 'objective' style which as Esther Newton argues reaffirms the hegemonic mode of disembodied academic discourse.

> ... by not 'problematising' (dreadful word, but none other works as well here) his own sexuality in his texts, the anthropologist makes make gender and heterosexuality the cultural given, the unmarked categories. If straight men choose not to explore how their sexuality and gender may affect their perspective, privilege, and power in the field, women and gays, less credible by definition, are suspended between our urgent sense of difference and justifiable fear of revealing it. (Newton, 1993, p 4)

Disembodied texts proclaiming the virtues of 'self-reflexivity' often seem ever destined to reach new heights of verbosity and new levels of abstraction in discussing metaphors of corporeality rather than their own actually existing sexual(ised) body. This theme is most eloquently reflected in Newton's statement that:

> Most reflexive" anthropology, which explicitly spotlights how ethnographic knowledge is produced, has rendered sex and emotion between ethnographers and informers more abstract than before. (Newton, 1993, p 5).

Whilst 'sexuality' and the 'body' may be 'en vogue' within certain components of the academic body concerned with social and cultural theory as witnessed by the plethora of new work; it is still rare to find actual accounts of sex and sexuality in the research process itself.

> We must begin to acknowledge eroticism, our own and that of others, if we are to reflect on its meaning for our work, and perhaps help alter our cultural system for the better, (Newton, 1993, p 8).

I am a gay man and as such my respondents are therefore potential sexual partners, Like Esther Newton,

> ... my key informants and sponsors have unusually been more to me than an expedient way of getting information, and

something different from 'just' friends. Information has always flowed to me in a medium of emotion - ranging from passionate erotic attachment to profound affection to lively interest - that empowers me in my projects and, when it is reciprocated, helps motivate informants to put with my questions and intrusions (Newton, 1993, p 11)

Esther Newton has argued that the erotic dimension has been notably absent from anthropological writing and Feminist anthropologists have been critical of the between intellect and emotion, mind and body dualism. Like Newton I would not want to overestimate the amount of power I had - most of the people I spoke to were from similar backgrounds to myself. Most were considerably better off, others were more highly educated. Few were impressed by my status, though most wanted to help me in my work, and were keen to understand what I would write about. Some were puzzled what the point was in doing the work. I was regarded as an oddball and eccentric academic whose choice of research topic reinforced their (severely misguided) impression of universities as bastions of liberal tolerance towards sexual divergence. They were generally supportive and open as answers to my research questions: how to make sense of being a gay man in the city; how to have sex in an epidemic, are to a certain extent their 'research questions' too. My research informants and myself were together speaking that language which Miller elucidates as that camp open-ended manner. Can one imagine most heterosexual men (or closeted gays) being so open about their sexuality as gay SMers?

> For me, intellectual and creative work, including fieldwork and the writing of ethnography, has always been inspired by, and addressed to, an interior audience of loved ones like informants and mentors. The most intense attractions have generated the most creative energy, as if the work were a form of courting and seduction (Newton, 1993, p 15)

I would strongly argue that we need to speak to each other and to our students in a language we can understand about AIDS and safer sex, because "how to have sex in an epidemic" is what they want and need to know; we have a duty to teach one another and inform them of the risks to create an embodied cultural geography of sexuality which deals with AIDS along the line of Tim Geltmaker's embodied geography of AIDS activism in Los Angeles (Geltmaker, 1992). Then our (sexualised) landscapes may be less marked by fear of death. What is ironic in the institutionalisation of lesbian and gay studies is that the blossoming of studies of texts and textuality has meant little discussion or mention of sex itself.

Concluding Remarks

One could be mistaken for believing that many academics don't have sex lives and are not embodied sexual beings who do form erotic attachments. One could be forgiven for thinking that sex only takes place in 'texts' and that disembodied metaphors of sex are all there is. In writing this piece I merely wish to challenge those who still maintain that emotions and (sexual) desires are merely a private affair, and that 'knowledge' is somehow a neutral, objective and public matter.

Acknowledgments

I would like to thank Minelle Mahtani, Ben Richards, Anson McKay, Peter Jackson, Jamie Crofts, Stephen Whittle and Julia Cream for reading and commenting on earlier versions of this chapter.

Bibliography

Bartlett, N. (1968) *Who Was That Man? A Present for Mr. Oscar Wilde*, Serpent's Tail, London.

Becker, H. (1986) *Writing for Social Scientists: How to Start and Finish Your Thesis, Book, or Article*, Chicago University Press, Chicago.

Bell, D., Binnie, J., Cream, J., and Valentine, G. (1994) "All Hyped Up and No Place to Go", in *Gender, Place and Culture: A Journal of Feminist Geography*, Volume 1, Number 1, pp 31-47.

Bibbings, L., Alldridge, P. (1993) "Sexual Expression, Body Alteration, and the Defence of Consent", *Journal of Law and Society*, Volume 20, Number 3, pp 356-370.

Brighton Ourstory Project (1992) *Daring Hearts: Lesbian and Gay Lives of 50s and 60s Brighton*, QueenSpark Books, Brighton.

Cooper, D. (1993) "An Engaged State: Sexuality, Governance, and the Potential for Change", *Journal of Law and Society*, Volume 20, Number 3, pp 257-275.

Fuss, D. (ed) (1992) *Inside/Out: Lesbian Theories/Gay Theories*, Routledge, London.

Geltmaker, T. (1992) "The Queer Nation Acts-Up: Health Care, Politics, and Sexual Diversity in the County of Angels", *Environment and Planning D: Society and Space*, 10, pp 609-650.

Goldsby, J. (1991) "What it Means to be Coloured Me", in Boffin, T., Fraser, J. (eds) *Stolen Glances: Lesbians Take Photographs*, Pandora, London.

Grant, L. (1993) *Sexing the Millennium*, Harper Collins, London.

Hoffman, E. (1991) *Lost in Translation : Life in a New Language*, Minerva, London.

Home, S. (1993) *No Pity*, AK Press, Edinburgh.

Home, S. (1991) *Defiant Pose*, Peter Owen, London.

Home, S. (1989) *Pure Mania*, Polygon, Edinburgh.

i-D Magazine, No.22 November 1993 *Carry on Class War!*, interview with Stewart Home.

Miller, D.A. (1992) *Bringing Out Roland Barthes*, University of California Press, Berkeley.

Newton, E. (1993) "My Best Informant's Dress: The Erotic Equation in Fieldwork", *Cultural Anthropology*, Volume 8, Number 1, pp 2-23.

Penley, C. (1992) "Feminism, Psychoanalysis, and the Study of Popular Culture", in Grossberg, L., Nelson, C., Treichler, P. (eds) *Culture Studies*, Routledge, London.

Piontek, S. (1992) "Unsafe Representations :Cultural Criticism in the Age of AIDS", *Discourse*, 15.1 (Fall 1992), pp 128-153.

Probyn, E. (1993) *Sexing the Self : Gendered Positions in Cultural Studies*, Routledge, London.

Ramazanoglu, C. (ed) (1993) *Up Against Foucault: Explorations of Some Tensions Between Foucault and Feminism*, Routledge, London.

Scott, J. (1992) "The Evidence of Experience", in Butler, J., Scott, J.W. (eds) *Feminists Theorize the Political*, Routledge, London.

Sedgwick, E.K. (1993) "Socratic Raptures, Socratic Ruptures: Notes Toward Queer Performativity", in Gubar, S., Kamholtz, J. (eds) *Inside and Out : The Places of Literary Criticism*, Routledge, London.

Shields, R. (1991) *Places on the Margin: Alternative Geographies of Modernity*, Routledge, London.

Tucker, S. (1991) "Gender, Fucking and Utopia", *Social Text*, 27.

Willis, S. (1993) "Hardcore: Subculture American Style", *Critical Inquiry* 19 (Winter 1993), pp 365-383.